W9-BLO-686

Dwarf Fruit Trees
Indoors and Outdoors

Dwarf Fruit Trees
Indoors and Outdoors

Robert E. Atkinson

VNR Van Nostrand Reinhold Company
New York Cincinnati Toronto London Melbourne

Van Nostrand Reinhold Company Regional Offices:
New York Cincinnati Chicago Millbrae Dallas
Van Nostrand Reinhold Company International Offices:
London Toronto Melbourne

Published by Van Nostrand Reinhold Company
450 West 33rd Street, New York, N.Y. 10001
Published simultaneously in Canada by
Van Nostrand Reinhold Limited
16 15 14 13 12 11 10 9 8 7 6 5 4 3 2 1

Contents

1 THE ASTOUNDING DWARFS

A full-size mature apple tree requires a space about 40 feet square. In the same amount of space, you could grow sixteen different types of dwarf trees with full-size fruit!

Dwarf fruit trees are appealing for other reasons as well. By planting several dwarfs the gardener can spread his risks, whereas in a small garden the death of one tree can wipe out his entire supply of fruit. If you are impatient, dwarfs are a good choice, for they bear fruit at an early age. Some are so precocious they produce fruit the same year they are planted, and most take only a year or two for bountiful yields; a standard tree takes five to ten years. In addition there are the incentives for growing fruit trees of whatever size or kind: the extra enjoyment to be had from plants that provide blooms in the spring and edible produce in the fall; the special savor of tree-ripened fruit; the pleasure of raising delicious and unusual varieties not grown commercially.

Misconceptions about dwarf trees have kept some gardeners from growing them. It is not true, for instance, that dwarfing a tree shortens its life. Sometimes the tiny trees are permitted to overbear, but with good care, dwarf apple and pear trees live for

Dwarf fruit trees in the foreground; standard varieties in the background.

seventy-five years, and other dwarf trees will have as many productive years as comparable standard-size trees.

Indoors, dwarf trees are the answer for "brown thumbers" who seek decorative plants able to survive adverse conditions. Citrus trees, with their bold green leaves and branching growth, make especially desirable accents for interiors. Dwarf trees are also at home as container plants on patios and terraces.

A vast new world of gardening awaits you when you raise dwarf fruit trees. They are rewarding plants with many uses both indoors and out, and in this book we hope to encourage you to grow and enjoy these astounding dwarfs.

HOW FRUIT TREES ARE DWARFED

Three methods are used to reduce the size of fruit trees: grafting or budding to a dwarfing root-stock, pruning, and growing in containers.

Grafting
Grafting is the dwarfing method used most frequently — about half the apple trees planted each year, for instance, are of the dwarf or compact types. They are developed by grafting or budding a desired

variety onto a special variety known as the rootstock; the rootstock restricts or dwarfs the growth of the scion (a shoot or a bud) grafted onto it. Roostocks are produced by cuttings from "hardwood" (stems of mature dormant shoots). The cuttings are taken in November, treated with a rooting hormone, and inserted into beds furnished with bottom heat. The cuttings root in a few months and are then planted in nursery rows in the spring and budded in August.

Citrus, apples, apricots, pears, peaches, quinces, plums, and sweet and sour cherries are the common fruits that can be dwarfed on special rootstocks.

Full-size flavorful fruit is one of the rewards of growing dwarf fruit trees. These fine pears are ready for picking.

Pruning

Summer pruning is necessary in gardens of full-size trees that have become too large. These trees may be cut back to mere stubs, forming bush-size trees, if such drastic treatment seems necessary. The fruiting branches are removed, of course, and a period of at least three years is necessary before the trees bear fruit again. However, old trees are often rejuvenated (if they survive). Commercial growers clip full-size orchard trees like a hedge or give the trees a "flat top" by cutting the top branches to the desired height. The sides often are cut at the same time or are trimmed in alternate years to prevent total interference with production.

Another technique for controlling ultimate size is called "branch bending." Yearly pruning establishes a central branch that is bent over; this branch induces early fruiting. New shoot growth is thus reduced, and the result is like a grape vine. This method may appeal to home gardeners; however, it still needs refinement, according to H. Jonkers of the University of Wageningen, the Netherlands. Research has revealed some problems: apple varieties suffer in fruiting habit if their branches are bent at a wrong angle. Keeping the right balance between shoot and fruit production is the key.

To facilitate spraying and picking, some growers prefer to make "hedgerows" of fruit trees by trimming them on opposite sides so that the trees are only 3 feet wide in their narrowest dimension. This preserves the fruiting wood on two sides, and the tree never goes completely out of bearing. It recovers quickly, and may ultimately produce almost as much fruit as a standard-size orchard tree.

Hedgerow fruit trees can be trained by driving a stake midway between four-year-old trees placed in a row. Baling twine is used to tie the limbs in a horizontal or downward sloping position, leaving only one central leader. Limbs growing into the row

'Yellow Delicious' apples on a dwarf tree. There is space in most gardens for such a tree, and the apples are certainly easy to pick. (Photo: Burpee Seeds)

Another reward — the lovely flowers. These belong to a 'Bonanza' dwarf peach.

are tied back into the hedge. (This training is tedious and expensive.) The trees are headed back at 12 feet and held at that height by pruning.

This method increases production; in a test made by the University of California, hedgerow pear plantings placed 11 feet apart (360 trees per acre) yielded over 8 tons per acre. Under similar conditions, regular-size trees on 20-foot centers (108 trees per acre) yielded less than 2 tons per acre. Picking and pruning operations were conducted by three men from the floor of a flat-bed trailer pulled by a tractor on platforms of high, medium, and low elevations. This elimination of ladders effected the greatest saving.

Time-and-motion studies at Oregon State University have shown that pickers spend two-thirds of their time on the ground or climbing ladders, and less than one-third actually picking fruit. European orchardists produce 15 tons per acre with the hedgerow method; the record yield is 25 tons.

Growing in Containers
Container gardening is popular now; it allows you to grow a plant where you want it, when you want it, and dwarf citrus make ideal container plants. The average mature dwarf tree is ideally suited to an 18 x 24-inch wooden tub; these are available at nurseries or you can make your own with redwood. Further, contained planting limits the size of the tree, keeping it to dwarf stature.

Growing plants in pots is no more work than growing them in the ground, and it may even be easier. You do not have to worry about the soil on your property, and if plants are getting too much sun or not enough, they can be moved. More information on container trees is given in the next two chapters.

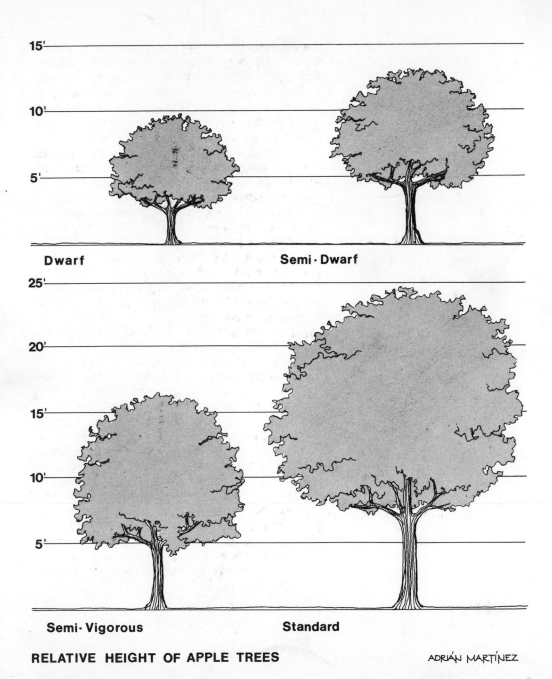

15'

10'

5'

Dwarf　　　　　　　　**Semi·Dwarf**

25'

20'

15'

10'

5'

Semi·Vigorous　　　　　**Standard**

RELATIVE HEIGHT OF APPLE TREES　　　ADRIÁN MARTÍNEZ

H.D.

2 GROWING FRUIT TREES INDOORS

A lime tree on your cocktail table or an orange tree in your kitchen will be the center of conversation whether you have a casual visitor or a huge party. Although oranges are associated with sunny California and Florida, and growing them indoors may seem an impossible feat, they are really amenable shade plants, often grown commercially under laths or in the shade of huge date palms. Thus the reduced light indoors is not a great disadvantage, although in cold-winter areas where the sun does not shine for long periods of time, you will have to provide the plants with as much light as possible.

You can grow dwarf oranges, lemons, or limes wherever you live, since all citrus are well adapted to being grown indoors. You can also grow figs and pomegranates—if you provide a greenhouse or atrium for them—but citrus are by far the most popular fruits for indoor culture.

Lemon trees that bloom continually and bear fruit in all stages of their development are especially rewarding, for the trees bear early—you will not have to wait three to five years to pick the first fruit. Crops are amazingly heavy for the size of the trees, and the fruit is not miniature but is as large as that borne on field trees. No other house plant can promise quite so much: handsome, shiny, evergreen foliage, fragrant flowers, *and* colorful and flavorful fruit.

Dwarf 'Gravenstien' apple

CONTAINER DWARFS IN HISTORY

Growing fruit trees in containers may seem a very modern idea, but it is as old as civilization. The ancient Greeks and Romans practiced pot culture, and the Persians used pots to transport trees from their native lands to one of the seven wonders of the ancient world, the hanging gardens of Babylon. Bas reliefs of fruit trees in containers are carved in the tombs of ancient Egyptian kings, and the use of "orangeries" (houses for citrus fruits grown indoors) became common in Europe following the Crusades.

Under the reign of Louis XIV boxed fruit trees were placed in heated greenhouses to force early production. The records of Louis' head gardener La Quintinya reveal that cherries were ripened in May and figs in June. In England, by about 1860, fruit culture in indoor containers flourished on a commercial scale. The danger of late-spring frosts was avoided, and the improved quality of the fruit, as well as the earliness, made the venture worthwhile.

This fine specimen orange tree prospers indoors all year. (Photo: Roche)

CARE OF CONTAINER DWARFS

Dwarf fruit trees are thus excellently suited for growing indoors, partly because growing in containers restricts the roots of plants, helping to keep them small; in fact, this is one of the recommended methods of dwarfing, as explained in Chapter 1. However, if you start with a dwarf tree in the first place, it is easier to keep the tree in bounds and to maintain its miniature size for several years without having to move it to a larger container.

There is nothing mysterious, nor are there any secrets, about the care of dwarf fruit trees indoors. The temperature of most homes (about 70°) is just right for most of these trees, and the dry air of centrally heated homes is not as great a menace to leather-leaved citrus trees as it is to many other indoor plants. Dwarf fruit trees are treated in much the same way you would tend many other standard houseplants, and with reasonable care they will prosper and become lovely decorative accents.

Containers
It is virtually impossible to grow citrus in a closed container. A good solution is to plant the citrus in a clay pot, and place the pot in an attractive jardiniere (redwood is a good material). The container should be about 14 to 18 inches square and 20 to 24 inches deep for most mature dwarf trees. Small plants from the nursery may be grown in 7-inch pots for about a year.

The container for your dwarf citrus tree should have casters so that the pot can be turned easily to obtain uniform light exposure. In Chapter 3 you will find more details on containers and how to make them portable.

Soil Mix

Correct planter mix is essential in the culture of container citrus; because the roots in the container have a smaller space from which to draw food, good soil is especially important. Citrus thrive on fertile loam soils but do best in quick-drying, well-drained soil. Sandy soils often hold so little water that it may prove difficult to maintain soil moisture. Peat moss holds too much water, and free water adjacent to mature roots may induce root rot. Where it is readily available, shredded fir bark can be used extensively. Sawdust shavings and similar wood products (except redwood) should be avoided because they decompose too quickly and cause a shortage of nitrogen. Washed cinders or silt-free sand can be mixed with soil and compost to provide a good growing medium.

A pH of 6.5 is most favorable, but trees will grow in alkaline soil if they are provided with trace minerals, especially iron, manganese, and zinc. Do not use manure or commercial fertilizer when planting.

Light

Although citrus trees can adapt to shade, they do best with a good supply of light. The amount of light that reaches a house plant, even in a picture window, is less than half that available outside the window. During short, dark winter days this may be too little light and is certain to be one-sided. Thus, the plant must be rotated to keep growth symmetrical. By utilizing reflectors you may increase the available light; use an aluminum or white backdrop or a nearby mirror or white-painted wall.

Remember that the sun changes its course during the year, and in winter the sun will stream into south windows. Similarly, the north window that gets little light in the winter may have full sun for an hour or more during the summer. Observe the particular conditions in your house and place your plants where they will receive most of the available sunlight.

A dwarf orange tree in a decorative bowl graces a living-room table.

Temperature

You must also provide the temperature requirements of the particular variety of dwarf citrus. Some need high temperatures for ripening; others do better under cool conditions. While most grapefruits, oranges, limes, and some mandarins can withstand temperatures over 100°F, if necessary, they prefer 70-75°F. Sudden temperature changes should always be avoided.

Humidity

Although citrus species will thrive under high humidity, they can withstand dry air. However, much more important is good air circulation around the plants. Do not place plants against a wall or in a windowless corner and expect them to grow — a dank enclosed situation is just as harmful as a constant draft.

Watering

Perhaps the greatest source of trouble in growing container citrus is overwatering. Citrus roots need an abundance of air, and when water is applied the air spaces in the soil are filled with water instead of air. As the soil dries, the air spaces become larger and larger, therefore anything you can do to extend the period between waterings, short of damaging the tree by allowing it to get too dry, will be beneficial. Optimum conditions for citrus roots occur in the period between waterings, so it is best to keep your established citrus trees on the dry side. The tree will tell you when it needs water — watch the leaves carefully. If they appear wan or limp, water the soil.

Cool temperatures and dry soil in winter will induce heavy flowerings as spring approaches. If water is hard, salts will build up in the soil like lime inside a teakettle; these salts must be flushed out of the soil by occasionally soaking the container in a bucket or tub of water for an hour or more until air bubbles appear on the soil, and then allowing the container to drain. Proper drainage and proper watering practices are as important as any other factor in ensuring success in the raising of dwarf citrus trees.

Fertilizing

Do not fertilize at planting time; wait six or seven months or until the citrus has become established. One level teaspoon of a 4- to 8-percent nitrogen fertilizer sprinkled over the surface and watered in is adequate for small plants. Late winter, June, and August are the best times. Be sure to fertilize after you flush excess salts from the soil. When new foliage is young, trace minerals such as iron, manganese, and zinc can be applied as a spray. Chelated minerals are most easily absorbed.

Pruning

Dwarf citrus need no pruning except for the removal of dead and crossing branches. Sometimes lemons will develop water sprouts; they should be pulled out at an early age. Light pruning to keep the tree the size desired will do no harm.

'Meyer' lemon, a container dwarf. (Photo: Clint Bryant)

Pollination

If fruit does not set when flowers are formed it may be because of a lack of pollination. Bees are essential to commercial fruit production; indoors, bees are not around to pollinate, and you may have to do the job yourself. Take a small cotton swab and rub it around the anthers (pollen-bearing sacks) of the opened flowers. Transfer the pollen (the yellow powdery dust) to the stigma (tip) of the pistil. The pistil is the knobbed central member of the flower that protrudes slightly above the ring of anthers that surrounds it. Do this when the stigma is sticky and moist, which indicates a receptive condition. However, most citrus trees produce fruits without pollination by means of "nucellar" fertilization: pollen is not functional, and the embryo is produced by an extrusion of the parent-tree tissue into the ovule that then develops into the seed. (This is the reason that most citrus seeds produce a tree identical to the parent.) The resulting plant is not dwarfed and must be grafted to limit its size.

CITRUS ON DWARFING ROOTSTOCK

The discovery that boosted the popularity of lilliputian citrus trees was the development of the dwarfing rootstock. By budding citrus to the trifoliate orange it was found that almost any citrus variety could be dwarfed. This breakthrough was pioneered by Mavro Warren of Piru and developed by Floyd C. Dillon and his son Don of Mission San Jose, California. The use of the special rootstock they developed is the key factor in dwarfing and requires painstaking selection for each citrus variety. The dwarfs produced from this rootstock develop fruits as desirable as any from the best orchard trees because the buds are selected from the most perfect strains. These dwarf trees not only require less space but are easier to pick and to check for pests. They are generally very productive in proportion to their small size. Their height is reduced by more than half when they are planted in the ground, and

they will rarely attain 6 feet in height, but growing in containers keeps them even more dwarf — usually less than 3 feet tall.

Sweet Oranges

The sweet oranges that can be produced in dwarf form are the navel, blood, and Valencia. 'Washington' navel is the most popular commercial variety and is America's favorite eating orange. It ripens eight to ten months after flowering, producing a large, seedless fruit that has a rather thick rind. 'Robertson' is a newer variety that bears heavily. It was derived from the 'Washington' and is the best-selling navel. 'Summer Navel,' as the name suggests, ripens in summer. It is a larger-leaved navel.

Blood oranges have red-shaded pulp and are widely grown in the Mediterranean basin. The amount of redness varies with the culture but is always highest in ripe fruit. 'Tarocco,' Italy's best strain, is available as a dwarf.

'Valencia' may need fifteen to nineteen months to ripen outdoors, but indoors it may be harvested in less than a year. 'Shamouti,' an Israeli variety, is almost seedless and ripens in the winter months. A variety called 'Seedless Valencia,' with excellent foliage and fruit, is also sold as a dwarf.

'Temple' is called a variety of orange, but its ancestry, although not definitely known, almost certainly must include the mandarin orange. 'Temple' ripens in February and March in warm areas but isn't ready until March or April in cool places. Unless kept warm in the winter it may fail to develop a sweet flavor.

A dwarf kumquat. (Photo: Clint Bryant)

Mandarins

All loose-skinned, thin-rind oranges are properly called mandarins, but they have come to be known popularly as tangerines. (The flattened varieties of mandarins are known as satsumas.)

The ideal mandarin for indoor culture is 'King,' but the tree tends to bear too heavily and sometimes only in alternate years. The large fruit has a bumpy, loose skin and ripens in the late spring. It needs high temperatures for good flavor. 'Kara,' a cross between 'King' and 'Satsuma,' has even larger fruit but fewer seeds, thinner rind, and pleasant-tasting meat. 'Kara' also needs high temperatures to ripen properly. Its broad leaves resemble those of the sweet orange.

The best-known tangerine is 'Dancy,' the deep-orange fruit available at Christmastime. The good flavor is developed in areas too cool for satsuma. 'Dweet,' a cross between 'Dancy' and the sweet orange, has large, very juicy fruit that ripens in the spring. 'Clementine,' which ripens earlier than 'Dancy,' has a richer flavor and needs less heat. 'Kinnow' is a hybrid between 'King' and 'Willow Leaf' and has beautiful foliage, but the fruit is full of seeds.

'Satsuma' varieties are all bud sports of one variety. The 'Owari' strain is the earliest ripening, but the fruit stays green until it over-ripens; then the skin becomes puffy. It is tender and nearly seedless. Usually the fruit is sweet, but it is rather tart when grown in a cool location. It ripens in November or December.

Grapefruits

The seedless 'Marsh' and the red-fleshed 'Ruby,' a sport of 'Marsh,' are the two grapefruit varieties that can be dwarfed from rootstocks. Most blossoms are produced in one season after a cool or dry period, with less out-of-season flowering than oranges, but where cool dry periods are not very long, grapefruits flower more often. In a cool room, grapefruits remain sour even after eighteen to twenty months on a tree; in hot locations they may ripen in nine months.

Crosses between mandarins (tangerines) and grapefruits are called tangelos. 'Minneola' has the richest flavor, is a little larger than an orange, and produces good flavor when grown in hot conditions. Its excellent tangerinelike fruits ripen in spring. 'Sampson' has yellow fruits that ripen in late spring when cultivated in a cool place; they are ready to pick in December and January if you grow them with sufficient heat. Some people prize tangelos above all other citrus fruits.

Lemons

The best-known market lemon is the 'Eureka,' which is nearly thornless. It prefers cool temperatures, and most of its fruit will ripen in summer. The hardier 'Lisbon' yields the bulk of its crop in the fall. It is much thornier but has greater vigor than 'Eureka.' The fruits are nearly identical.

'Ponderosa' lemon has fruits often weighing 2 pounds each. Although large, these fruits are juicy and full of flavor and are excellent for pies. The thorns are a drawback, but fortunately 'Ponderosa' needs much less light than other citruses, and in reduced light it may be the only one that will produce flowers and fruit.

Although lemon trees bloom year-round, most of their flower production is in the spring.

A 'Rangpur' lime. (Photo: Clint Bryant)

Limes

Two types of limes are commonly grown. One originated in India and was introduced into the New World by the Spaniards. It now grows wild in Mexico and is known as 'Mexican' lime. The tree is smaller and bushier than most citrus, with smaller leaves and very seedy fruit. Another type, known as 'Tahiti,' has larger fruit; it may have originated in Persia. 'Bearss' is from the 'Tahiti' strain and is virtually seedless and extremely vigorous. It rarely produces viable pollen. Like lemons, limes bloom most of the year, with heaviest bloom following a period of cool temperatures or a dry period. Spring blooms develop into ripe fruit by Christmas but may be earlier if indoor temperatures are high in the summer. Maximum size may be attained only 130 days after flowering. Both 'Mexican' lime and 'Tahiti' have much juice and rich lime flavor. Their fruit ripens throughout the year.

'Rangpur' is called a lime (the continual blooming habit and small flowers indicate that it is part lime), but the ease with which it segments suggests that it is related to the mandarin orange. Curiously, the flower petals are darker than those of the mandarin, but lime flowers are pure white. The leaves resemble lime foliage. The flavor is rich and highly acid but less acid than true limes.

Limequats are hybrids of limes and kumquats. The fruit is limelike, and the rind edible, as with the kumquat. Flowering is almost entirely limited to a single flush in the spring. 'Eustis' is available on a dwarfing rootstock.

THE NATURAL DWARFS

'Meyer' lemon

The best natural dwarf is 'Meyer' lemon, a genetic dwarf that is perhaps a hybrid of lemon and orange, since it has characteristics of both. Discovered in the Orient by the plant explorer Frank N. Meyer, it was grown for centuries in China. It has been available here for years. The beautiful dense foliage is almost thornless, and the fruit is smooth, thin-skinned and light-orange in color. The juice is golden-yellow, plentiful, and of medium acidity. It is a precocious bloomer: one-year-old trees often set fruit. Flowers and fruit generally appear on the tree throughout the year. Fruit is smaller when grown on a dwarfing rootstock.

'Otahiete' orange

'Otahiete' orange is a misnomer, for the fruit of this natural dwarf resembles a lime more than an orange. The fruits, only 2 inches in diameter, are in excellent scale for a pot plant. They are mainly decorative, however, for the fruit is flavorless. The plant is easily grown from cuttings. It is nearly thornless, and begins bearing when less than 1 foot tall.

'Chinotto' orange

'Chinotto' is a sour-orange variety that produces a profusion of small, round, deep-orange-colored fruit. The fruit lasts for long periods and contrasts with the fine foliage. This plant is especially decorative at Christmastime, for it may bear a dozen ripe fruits.

A 'Pyrus' kawakami. (Photo: Clint Bryant)

Calamondins

Calamondins have been grown indoors for centuries. They have round fruit about the size of a ping-pong ball and remain green when ripe. Very prolific, calamondins bear fruit all year, and one small tree can produce hundreds of fruits. Although the fresh pulp has a slightly soapy taste, the juice can be used like lemons and limes to make a refreshing drink or to flavor fish and other foods. Calamondins can be kept below 2 feet in height by light pruning in the spring and summer.

Kumquats

The kumquat is a variety of citrus that is related to the rue family. The plants are naturally small, but when grafted on a trifoliate orange rootstock they are even more dwarfed. The leaves are one-fourth to one-half the size of orange leaves and are more pointed. Fruits, which are seldom more than 1 inch in diameter, are of a bright-orange color and have a rind that is thick, fleshy, sweet, and spicy. The entire fruit is eaten — peel and all. Kumquats make excellent pickles and marmalades; the candied fruits are a gourmet's treat. In China, potted kumquat trees are placed on the dining table, and the fruit is eaten between courses.

The fruit holds well on the plant and thus may be found in almost any month, although fall to midwinter is the season for ripening fruit. 'Nagami' is the best-known variety. A very dwarf species, F. hindsii, a rare collector's item, produces large numbers of tiny fruits and is called 'Golden Bean' by the Chinese.

Unless you live in such subtropical areas as California, Florida, or Hawaii (where you can purchase your trees locally in gallon cans or balled and burlaped), you will have to order plants by mail. Keep in mind, however, that state laws forbid shipment from California into Florida or from any state into California.

RAISING FRUIT TREES FROM SEED INDOORS

You can plant your own citrus. The next time you eat an orange or grapefruit (or any other citrus), save the seeds and plant them in a pot of coarse, organic planter mix. Place a pane of glass over the top of the pot so that you won't have to water it continually. The seed will germinate and develop into a tree that will stay small as long as its roots are restricted by a pot. Unlike most fruits, citrus seeds usually come true to type. But in the juvenile condition that persists for several years, the tree may be excessively thorny. Flowering and fruit production by seedlings is usually much delayed compared to grafted plants.

Other dwarf fruits that can be grown indoors, as noted at the beginning of this chapter, are figs and pomegranates. You can also have a lot of fun growing dates, mangoes, papayas, and avocados from seed, but don't expect fruit.

A 'Mineola' tangelo. (Photo: Clint Bryant)

3 INDOOR/OUTDOOR TREES

Trees grown in containers can be enjoyed both indoors and outdoors, even in cold-winter areas. In these areas, evergreen citrus are grown indoors and can be moved outdoors in warm weather; deciduous fruit trees, on the other hand, are grown in containers to be kept outside most of the time and moved indoors for short periods to serve as decoration.

All types of deciduous fruit trees can be grown in containers. The new, natural dwarf peaches and nectarines are an excellent choice for use in this way. They are very decorative and are sometimes grown for their foliage and flowers alone. In the winter they offer a somber study of bare brown branches studded with fruit and leaf buds; spring brings a giant bouquet; and in the summer there are hidden surprises among the dense foliage. These are plants you will never have to relegate to an out-of-the-way corner, for their beauty is constant. And by moving them indoors during freezing spring nights when they are in bloom, you can grow peaches in years when the local peach crop is killed by frost.

Deciduous fruit trees should be displayed indoors only for a special evening or weekend — rarely for a week or longer. The leaves may drop, from the lack of humidity in heated rooms or from a lack of light, which causes an abscission layer to form in the leaf stalk, as it does in the autumn before the leaves fall. Light, of course, is the limiting factor; if you have a bright atrium, greenhouse, or sunroom with a skylight, you might be able to grow the evergreen tropical fruits year-round. (These fruits include papaya, guava, sapote, and all citrus.)

However, all deciduous fruit trees need a certain amount of winter chilling to break dormancy; if cold is lacking, the trees struggle to bloom erratically and new leaves are produced over a long period. Since most deciduous trees are not very decorative in the winter, two purposes will be served if you move the plants to a protected spot outside and await the return of their leaves in the spring.

If you live where pears, apricots, peaches, cherries, and Japanese plums are not hardy, you can grow them by moving them into a garage or shed for several months during the winter and giving them protection from freezing when they are in bloom.

Fruit trees moved indoors while they are blooming will have to be hand-pollinated if they are to produce fruit. The procedure for pollinating these trees is the same as that for citrus, as described in Chapter 2.

This lovely dwarf kumquat spends its summers outdoors, winters indoors, where it is a decorative room accent.

PRUNING

Severe pruning is especially important for container culture. Thinning out and heading back must be done constantly so that the form is maintained. The taller dwarfs that may be grown in pyramid form includes apples, pears, cherries, and apricots; they should be headed at 30 inches. Peaches, nectarines, plums, and cherries adapt to bush form; they should be headed as low as 9 to 12 inches. Pinching of the shoots during the growing season reduces the amount of winter pruning needed.

LIMITING FRUIT PRODUCTION

Apricot, plum, and cherry trees should be limited to about twenty-five fruits the first bearing year; all other trees should be allowed to produce only ten fruits.

TYPES OF CONTAINERS

Plant containers should always be in proportion to the size of the plant. They may be made of clay, porcelain, wood, concrete, fiberglass, plastic, or metal. All containers must have drainage holes unless they will serve as jardinieres (good-looking jars that hold the actual containers).

Each material has its advantages, but clay (terra cotta) is nearly ideal because the porous nature of the clay allows air to reach the roots from all sides. However, the natural red color may be quickly stained by lime or soil. Unglazed terra cotta pots dry out more rapidly; thus plants need water more often, especially in dry weather.

Glazed or porcelain jars are nonporous and are easier to clean than clay; thus they are excellent for jardinieres. If the jar has a wide mouth, an unglazed clay pot may be inserted and the space between the walls of the pot and the jar filled with peat moss.

This method is called "double potting" and allows you to water a plant correctly without having water drain onto the rug or the floor of the patio. You can water the plant thoroughly, for all excess water is absorbed by the peat moss. (Never water if the peat moss is wet.)

Perhaps the best patio containers are those made of wood, such as boxes, tubs, and half-barrels. The greatest advantage of wood is its porous nature. This provides an insulation that prevents roots, which wind around the outside of the soil bar next to the container wall, from being cooked by the high temperatures that develop when sunlight strikes directly on containers placed outdoors. A metal or plastic container, on the other hand, will absorb the heat and damage the roots.

Redwood, cedar, and cypress are excellent woods for containers because they resist rotting by fungi and they age beautifully, with little or no stain or other finish required. Douglas fir and pine can be given a coat of a wood preservative, and wood stain will keep them attractive. If you use plywood, be careful to use the outdoor type. Wood boxes can be made easily, and various patterns and designs can be obtained from your local lumber dealer.

The new fiberglass containers made by Architectural Fiberglass Company of Los Angeles, California, offer solid-appearing planter boxes in pleasing shapes and designs; they come in sizes large enough to hold little patio plants. These containers are very lightweight and have a double wall that prevents temperatures from adversely affecting the plant roots.

A clay container is ideal for a small tree like this dwarf orange. (Photo: Doherty Associates, Inc.)

HOW TO MOVE CONTAINERS

From time to time you will need to move heavy trees in large containers. A heavy container can be pushed over level ground on three pieces of pipe: two are laid under the box while the third is moved ahead. This device may be used to cross lawns or soft gravel if a board track is laid first.

Permanent casters or small wheels can be attached to heavy containers, or you can buy a dolly or stand on casters to fit the container. If you buy only one dolly and have several boxes to move, you must be able to lift the planter box onto the dolly. You can build a rack or litter from 2 x 4 lumber (this forms the handles), and an 18-inch square of ½-inch plywood nailed to one end will stabilize the rack. With this device, two men can move a 200-pound planted box and tree. A hand truck such as a professional mover uses is best for moving up or down stairs.

Smaller containers can be moved by skidding on a burlap bag or a piece of an old rug. A long-handled flat shovel can be used to drag a tub across a lawn or cement surface; the blade under the tub serves as a skid and reduces friction.

PLANTING IN CONTAINERS

Cover each drain hole with a curved piece of broken clay pot. Do not place gravel in the bottom; chips of wood or bark may be used to facilitate drainage. Fill the bottom with damp planter mix.

Before planting in a wooden container, soak the container thoroughly to fill the pores with water. Otherwise, the soil will lose moisture to the wood and shrink away from the sides, allowing the water applied to drain around the soil ball without actually wetting it.

'Bonanza' peach in a wooden container can be moved about the patio.

Dwarf kumquat in a glazed container.

Planter Mix

All fruit trees will thrive on a soil composed of one-third peat moss, one-third perlite, and one-third soil. Add 3 pounds of a balanced 6-10-4 fertilizer to a cubic yard of this mix and 1 pound of hoof-and-horn meal. Set the plant on a layer of mix, with the original soil line about 2 inches from the top of the container. Fill around the plant with planter mix, and tamp with a dibble stick (a short, blunt wooden stick, such as a piece of hoe handle). Apply water to the top of the soil, and allow it to settle. Repeat until no further settling occurs and water drips from the drain holes.

A planter mix containing a large proportion of perlite and peat moss will be lighter than one containing soil, and in watering you will add much weight; so be sure to move the container to its permanent place before you water it.

Repotting

You can promote the small tree from a 1-foot-square container after two or three years. After the third or fourth move, it should be in a 24-inch box. Move the tree in the spring, before the leaves appear. Water heavily the day before moving, and, using an old saw, loosen the sides of the root ball from the box. Lay the box on its side, and ease the plant onto an old rug or piece of burlap by pulling on its trunk. (If the plant sticks, a couple of sharp blows on the box with a mallet will loosen it quickly.) Remove one-third of the soil from the root ball, and cut back the larger roots by one-third their length. Replace with fresh planter mix, and set at the same depth as before.

If space permits, transfer your potted tree after ten years to a permanent location in the ground and start again with a new, small tree.

Wooden containers such as this are available at almost any nursery or gardening-equipment store. Note that the tub rests on blocks to promote drainage.

'Bonanza' peach blooming in rustic redwood container.

H.D.

4 PLANNING AND PLANTING OUTDOORS

Dwarf trees grown exclusively for fruit can be used as important elements in the landscape, for even without fruit, they are extremely beautiful, ornamental plants. Their landscaping role is frequently overlooked, but if you will examine the trees in blossom, their form and shape, foliage characteristics, and the bark and twigs when the trees are dormant, you will see that they are excellent decorative material.

As an accent in the garden or for group plants, they are attractive. And they make excellent hedges or screens. Dwarf fruit trees also excel as espaliers where they appear attractive in the landscape plan. Where cultural conditions can be met (see Chapter 6), they are certainly desirable trees.

LANDSCAPING WITH DWARF TREES

Plantings will be enjoyed most if they are grouped in pleasing masses in the landscape. Too many specimen plants, each set off by themselves, result in a cluttered appearance. One or two especially beautiful plants, however, may be used as accents. Pairs of identical fruit trees may emphasize architectural features such as front entrances, garden paths, or flights of steps, but the repeated use of pairs makes for uninteresting design.

Dwarf kumquat

First plan group planting on paper. Select a tall or imposing variety, and space around it shorter varieties that complement and enhance the main choice. Sometimes three similar-sized fruit trees may be planted in one large hole to give a variety of fruit over a longer period of time; such groupings are often well placed at a corner of the lot or at the corner of the house.

If you want fruit trees near the house, plant them far enough away from the house so that when they are fully grown you can easily walk between the house and the planting. This arrangement offers better light conditions on all sides and makes spraying and pruning easier. It also allows good air circulation, which will help to keep your trees free from mildew and other diseases.

Groups should not be laid out in rigid, angular patterns; beds that are gently curved have a more pleasing appearance. Before planting use a hose to create the outline of the bed. If you choose low-growing dwarfs, little pruning will be necessary. Repeat the exact planting on the opposite corner for a formal, symmetrical design; but for a more sophisticated, asymmetrical balance, choose different types of plants arranged so that the mass appears to balance the planting on the other side.

A perfectly balanced landscape will appear dull and uninteresting without accents. Fruit trees, by

their spectacular nature, can be used admirably to relieve monotony of line or color and to give a dominant focal point to the design.

Dwarf fruit trees also can be used as hedges or screens, or they may be spaced to delineate the property line. They are pleasing if placed along a driveway, for the seasonal changes may be observed daily as you drive in and out. And on a fall day when breakfast is missed or incomplete, you can sample your own produce.

One of the best uses of fruit trees is in espaliers to decorate fences and walls. All the finer details of a plant are thus displayed — the line of stem, the color and texture of bark and foliage, and the beauty of flower and fruit. Espaliers will be described in the next chapter.

Shape and Sizes of Trees

The sizes and shapes of dwarf trees vary considerably. Pears are of medium size and are inclined to be pyramidal; apples, about the same ultimate size, are rounded. Plums, apricots, and most cherries produce large trees with rounded heads, but the 'Morello' cherry may have an almost weeping aspect. Apricots and plums will often be large enough to use as shade trees.

The tiny, natural dwarf peaches are shrublike and should be seen throughout the year, for each season brings a changing aspect. A good location is on a steep hillside near your house. The trees will make a spectacular display as the double pink blossoms appear. From the time the leaves appear until late December, the trees are clothed with dark-green foliage that almost hides the developing fruit.

Foliage

Although the leaves of various fruit trees are much alike in texture, they differ in other ways. The long, narrow, willowlike foliage of peaches and Japanese plums contrast sharply with the oval or round leaves of apples, pears, plums, and cherries. The leaves of some varieties are dark green; others are light green. Fall foliage color also is interesting: some pears have flaming red leaves, and the leaves of sweet cherries often turn bright yellow before they drop.

In winter the deciduous fruit trees acquire a different aspect, when the unique beauty of their bare twigs, branches, and trunks is revealed. The bark of cherries and plums is smooth and reddish; that of peaches and Japanese plums is light-brown or yellowish-brown. Apricots and plums have gray bark, as do apples and pears. The picturesque, crooked quinces are a feature of the winter landscape, as are pears, and the fine tracery of plum and cherry branches casts a network of spidery shadows on the snow.

Flowers

Fruit trees in bloom offer a spectacular display of color that rivals many flowering shrubs. Pears, plums, and cherries are masses of white, and peaches and apples usually bloom in shades of pink. The flowering season in the New York area begins the last of April and, with a good selection of varieties, continues until late May.

Fragrance

Fragrance is one of the qualities that should be considered when planning the placement of trees. Apples can be planted adjacent to the patio or to bedroom windows so that you can enjoy their perfume without entering the garden. Other fruit trees have less fragrance; the pear has little or none.

A single dwarf tree can give a garden a charming focal point.

A specimen orange tree screens a driveway area.

An orchard of dwarf fruit trees.

Fruit

The landscape value of ripening crabapples, cherries, and plums is quiet apparent. Less striking are the fruits of apples, pears, and peaches, for they are partly hidden by the foliage. But red or yellow apples on a small tree are an exciting sight, and golden pears and peaches make splendid pictures. However, plums offer the widest range of sizes and colors, from clear yellow through blue and purple to deep red. Cherries, too, offer much contrast, from the white-fruited types to the dark, almost black, varieties.

Evergreen Citrus for Warm Climates

In the warm-winter areas, evergreen dwarf citrus are highly prized as landscape elements, aside from the beauty and utility of their fruit. Most of these citrus have shiny, dark green leaves, and the flowers, although not particularly showy, add a bit of contrasting white that sets off the foliage. The fragrance of citrus flowers is outstanding, and lemon and calamondin may be enjoyed all year. Oranges tend to bloom heavily in spring; most limes bloom in the fall. (See Appendix for other fruiting and blooming times.)

The sour orange *Citrus aurantium* has been used extensively as a street tree in Arizona because the ornamental fruits are so sour that they are not picked by vandals. Specimens of the 'Bouquet' orange, a natural dwarf, rarely grow higher than 8 to 10 feet and are especially well adapted to growth as standards with the top pruned in a spherical shape. Thus treated, they are useful for decorating entrances and as corner accents. The 'Bouquet' orange and the 'Chinotto,' which bears smaller fruits, have been used extensively as hedges. The fingered citron, another natural dwarf, grows easily from cuttings and is prized for its fragrant fruits that may be used as sachets.

In Florida the calamondin orange on dwarfing rootstock is a popular landscape tree because its fruits are smaller and more in scale with a miniature tree. Its continuous bloom and fruit make it exceptionally ornamental. The 'Meyer' lemon and other lemons on dwarfing rootstocks are popular in California for use in espaliers. They, too, have the advantage of continuous bloom and fruit.

PLANNING AN ORCHARD

If you have sufficient space you may want to plant an orchard. Choosing an orchard site is a most exciting experience, to be savored throughout the cold winter — by day, the area is measured and surveyed, and by night the varieties are selected and the planting plan made.

The ideal choice for an orchard is a gently sloping, sunny rectangular plot with slightly acid, fertile, well-drained soil. (It must be well-drained, since planting fruit on poorly drained soil is a waste of money.) Most important is the lack of competition from overhanging foliage and from the roots of trees and shrubs. The location of the orchard, if a choice is available, should be convenient to the house.

In planning the home orchard, high yields, shipping quality, and appearance are minor considerations. Fine flavor is most important, and if storage space is available, keeping quality should also be considered.

Apples, pears, quinces, peaches, apricots, plums, and cherries can be grown almost anywhere. In a ¼-acre plot (80 x 65 feet) you can grow nine kinds of apples, six kinds of pears, four sour and four sweet cherries, six kinds of peaches and nectarines, three apricots, ten kinds of plums, or one quince. (See chart following.)

These trees should be spaced roughly at 10 square feet per tree. This plan will not exactly fit the conditions in any specific case, but it shows the number of varieties you can grow in a small space.

TYPE	ROOT STOCK	FEET APART IN ROW	WIDTH OF ROWS
APPLE			
	EM IX	6–8	10–12
	EM VII	12	20
	Spur types	12	12
PEAR			
	'Anger C'	6–8	10
	'Anger A'	12	15
CHERRY			
	Sour	15	15
	Sweet	20	25
	'North Star'	10	10
PEACH			
	Natural dwarfs	6	6
	'Plum'	15	15
	'Apricot'	15	25

Note that in the plan the fruits are planted in blocks to facilitate spraying and pollination; the cherries are planted on inside rows to lessen damage caused by birds.

Frost Injury

If frost is a problem, and it usually is, trees should be located on a slope with good air drainage. Cold air is heavy and will sink to the lowest spot. This is especially important in planning the location of dwarf trees, for their flowers are closer to the ground than the flowers of standard trees. If thirty or more dwarf trees are planted to the acre, the movement of air will be impeded, making frost damage more likely.

Tissues that are growing actively can be killed by temperatures slightly below 32°F, the freezing point of water. Freezing may occur in the early fall when late fertilization, watering, or warm temperatures keep stems in active growth past the time of normal dormancy. However, most frost damage occurs in the spring when growth is just starting. Flower buds are very susceptible to injury, but young fruits are even more susceptible to frost than are flowers in full bloom. Thus early-blooming fruit trees (apricots and peaches) cannot be counted on for crops where late frosts occur regularly. A temperature of 30°F can damage young apricot fruit, but open flowers often withstand 20°F temperatures without injury. Late-flowering apple varieties such as 'Rome Beauty' and 'Northern Spy' can succeed in areas where late frosts occur.

Frost injury is easy to identify. The pistil (central element) of the flower turns black, and in forty-eight hours the seed inside an injured fruit will turn brown. Such fruits will soon fall from the tree.

Citrus trees can withstand 15°F without dying, and the leaves survive temperatures as low as 22°F, but fruits are damaged by temperatures below 25°F. Lemons, the most susceptible to frost, cannot withstand temperatures below 30°F.

There are many ways of protecting blooming fruiting trees from frost. The easiest is to throw a cover, such as a blanket or other opaque material, over them. This prevents the loss of heat from the soil by radiation, which is the primary cause of freezing damage. A better method is to make a framework to hold a cover well over the top of the plant. The cover need not extend down to the soil, but if it does, the plant is better protected in intense cold. The best method is to place a burning electric light bulb under the cover; this will keep the temperatures inside the tent above freezing even if the thermometer outside registers 20°F.

Winter Injury

Winter injury is quite different from frost damage. Usually it occurs on trunks and branches with smooth bark that receives the full impact of the winter sun. This type of damage is always on the sunny side of the tree and may be quite extensive or very limited. Such damage usually occurs late in the winter when tissues are about to begin their spring growth. The warm rays of the winter sun trick the tissues under the bark into growth; thus, in their most susceptible condition, the tissues succumb to freezing temperatures. The damage may be controlled by whitewashing, thus protecting the surfaces exposed to the sun.

Trunks badly damaged by winter injury usually have cracks appearing in the bark; the bark separates from the wood. A killing back of twigs at the top of the tree is another symptom. Badly damaged trees usually grow out of the injury and recover completely.

Do not cut back dead or injured limbs until early summer. By that time, all living tissues have had an opportunity to grow and new shoots have developed. Cut out all dead wood, but do not start shaping the tree until the following fall or winter. Severe pruning of winter-damaged trees and removal of new shoots may weaken them further.

Peach-flower buds in the dormant condition die at temperatures of −15°F, which is the prime reason for the limited range of this fruit. The hardiest varieties can withstand temperatures below this. Figs die when temperatures drop below zero, but apples, pears, most plums, peaches, and apricots can survive −30°F.

Dwarf fruit trees are available at nurseries in cans.

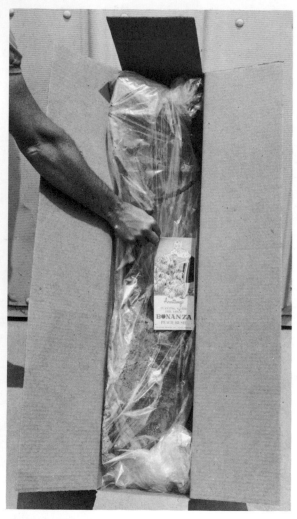

A good mail-order nursery will package plants carefully so that they will arrive in good condition anywhere in the country.

Some varieties are available neatly packaged and ready for planting.

Windbreaks

Protection from wind damage is an important consideration in raising dwarf fruit trees because

1. The trees are not as deeply rooted as standard trees and are therefore not as well anchored.
2. Some rootstocks are brittle and may break.
3. Trees are inclined to overgrow and make heavy tops, causing them to topple in strong winds.
4. Free-standing hedgerow plantings set at right angles to the prevailing wind are predisposed to damage.
5. Heavy maturing fruit may be shaken off by windstorms.

The best protection from wind that comes mostly from one direction (prevailing wind) is a windbreak. A row of shrubs or trees is effective; evergreens (conifers) are more effective than deciduous shrubs or trees. If no windbreak is available, fruit trees closely planted in rows afford considerable protection to each other.

Staking and Bracing

Single trees can be given protection from prevailing winds by planting them at a slight slant into the wind, by staking, by bracing with wire braces, or by a combination of these methods. Some varieties need staking more than others. (See Chapter 6.) Trees in poor soil have less abundant root growth and may lean or blow over if not staked.

Proper pruning practices can reduce the need for staking. By heading low and encouraging branches on the windward side, extensive root development will be produced on that side and will stabilize the tree in the wind.

A young tree usually needs bracing; the easiest way is to tie an oblique stake to the trunk. The stake need not be driven in deeply as proper positioning against the prevailing wind is sufficient to stabilize the tree. Guy wires, or a single vertical stake of steel or wood to which the tree is fastened, may also be used. Wire tied with pieces of old garden hose, and old steel fence posts are still other ways to brace the tree (but 2 x 2 redwood stakes are more handsome in the garden).

Never use unprotected wire or twine for tying; it will cut the tree. A green plastic tape that breaks when growth pressure is exerted has recently been developed and is satisfactory. Excellent ties can be made with loops, or strips of old inner-tubes (one turn around the stake, and one around the stem) can be fastened to the wooden stake with a stapler. A rubber tie, notched at one end and slit at the other, is now available; the notched end is slipped through the slit to make a secure tie.

SOIL

Almost any kind of soil is suitable for growing fruit trees, but very light and very heavy soils will be more troublesome. The most important requirement is good drainage. Pears, plums, quinces, and apples are less sensitive to high moisture, but wet soil is bad for all fruit trees. Sometimes rootstocks may be chosen that are more tolerant of wet soil. The dwarfing-apple understocks named Malling I, VII, IX, XIII, and XVI tolerate heavy soils, and EM IV, II, and MM 104 thrive in lighter soil. EM VII seems to be tolerant of the widest range of soil-moisture variation.

Poor soil-drainage is most often evident in the winter when water accumulates and stands for long periods. It can be alleviated by laying 3-inch drainage tile at a depth of 3 feet (or deeper), draining to the lowest spot in the area. The depth of the soil is not important (except to provide drainage). Fruit trees have shallow roots, and the roots of dwarf trees seldom penetrate deeper than 3 feet.

The pH measure of the soil — its acidity or alkalinity — must also be considered. A pH of 7 is neutral, below 7 is acid, and above 7 is alkaline. Soil that is acid (pH 4.5) is suitable for cranberries and blueberries but not for dwarf fruit trees. A pH of 5.5-6.5 is ideal for these trees. To get good fruit crops in the Southwest, soils too alkaline (pH 7.5-8) must be treated with soil sulfur that is well-mixed into the soil at planting time.

You will find trees growing in soil that has a higher or lower pH than recommended, but these plants would do better and need less fertilizer if the soil reaction were adjusted. Plants are affected by acidity or alkalinity because these conditions make some necessary nutrient elements insoluble and unavailable to plants. An application of these elements will temporarily relieve the deficiency, but for permanent, inexpensive correction, apply lime to correct acidity, and apply sulfur to correct alkalinity. These remedies should be used as needed, after an accurate soil test has been made by a reputable firm.

Preparing the Soil

Soil fertility has more to do with the structure of the soil than with the presence or absence of fertilizer elements that can be supplied at low cost. However, if the soil structure is poor, the cost of these amendments (excessive for the orchardist because he has so many trees) may be practical for the home gardener.

Humus is the essence of fertile soil. If soils are too light and sandy or are too heavy because they contain too much silt or clay, the addition of humus in the form of compost will make them fertile.

It takes prodigious amounts of compost to alter the soil structure, especially when soil is too heavy. You cannot use raw organic matter; it must be partially digested or decomposed to be of any value. Manures containing raw straw or shavings are beneficial when used on top of the soil as a mulch, but they may cause plants to turn yellow from a lack of nitrogen if they are incorporated into soil.

It is necessary to improve the soil only in the immediate vicinity of dwarf trees. Thoroughly decomposed compost used in the planting hole is usually sufficient if the soil is of average condition.

Beware, however, of planting in a hole in which the roots are restricted by unimproved, compacted soil. A sharp change from improved to unimproved soil is called an interface, and this impedes the penetration of roots. A plant whose roots are limited by an interface grows like one in a container and thus needs all the extra attention container plants require.

WHEN TO PLANT

Fall is the best time to plant in areas where winters are not severe and where dormant nursery stock can be obtained. The cool soil favors abundant root growth, and cold air temperatures hold back tops so that the trees are well established when the spring surge of growth occurs. Where winters are severe and winter injury and winter kill are a hazard, spring planting is recommended. Plant the trees as soon as the holes can be dug. If nursery stock arrives too early, it can be "heeled in" in a bed of moist shavings or straw.

ORDERING THE STOCK

The cost of individual trees is such a small part of the cost of getting a mature tree to bearing size that bargains should be carefully scrutinized. Never buy unseen nursery stock from itinerant salesmen, even if offered at low prices. The established firms that stand behind their varietal names guarantee freedom from virus diseases and furnish healthy, rooted plants, giving the best bargains regardless of price.

The nature of the rootstock is just as important as the variety. Therefore, buy stock only when the rootstock is named and guaranteed. The size of the plant is less important than its quality and condition, but very small trees may be inherently weak. Insist on No. 1 grade for best results.

Dwarf trees are not to be confused with weak trees. Bare root and balled and burlaped stock should be sturdy and of good caliper (trunk diameter). They should be at least two years old; some trained espaliers may be four to eight years old. Older trees do not ship well except in containers, and espaliers that have been started should be purchased from a nearby nursery so that they can be dug and transplanted the same day.

HOW TO PLANT

The size of the planting hole depends on the productivity (natural fertility) of the soil. In the average garden a hole large enough to accommodate the roots without crowding or bending is ample. In poor soil, a hole 3 x 3 feet wide and 2 feet deep is not too large; save the topsoil and mix it with compost or well-rotted manure. Return this mixture to the bottom of the hole, and use it around the roots as fill. Do not use commercial fertilizer at this time.

Before planting, cut off the fine roots that have become dried out in shipping. Then prune broken or damaged roots, and shorten the extra long roots that don't fit into the hole. Set the tree high enough to prevent any danger of the scion rooting. With the plant held firmly in place, return the soil mixture to the hole, stamping down firmly with your feet to hold the tree erect and to settle the soil.

Do not hill up the soil around a newly planted tree; instead, make a basin the width of the planting hole to facilitate watering. If the soil is dry, water thoroughly.

First the dwarf fruit tree is set in an excavated hole with prepared soil. The hole is filled with fresh soil, and tamped to remove air pockets. Then the soil is thoroughly watered. After about twenty minutes, when the water has soaked in, the soil should be watered again.

PRUNING AT PLANTING TIME

Pruning a young tree gives it a framework of scaffold branches that holds the fruit without breaking. There is no harm from heavily pruning a tree at planting time (and most trees received from the nursery require much attention). Removing wood at this time benefits the roots and helps the tree to become established before the top develops more leaves than the damaged roots can sustain.

Apples and Pears

Two-year-old trees have several lateral branches. At planting time, head low apples on EM IX, and select scaffolds that are between 1 and 2 feet on the trunk. Leave a branch as low as 6 inches above ground, but remove it later. Sometimes nurserymen rub off buds below 2 feet while the tree is in the nursery, but this should not be done for dwarf trees. If buds are present, cut back to a height of 2 to 2½ feet. Any laterals present that are spaced right can be cut to one-third or one-half their length and retained; all others should be removed. Usually, branches are not spaced and formed ideally, or at best only one is, in which case all undesirable ones should be removed.

Most trees on dwarfing rootstocks are started from a whip, and the buds are forced to form a low head. Remove all blossoms or fruits the first year unless you wish to retain one or two for show. The next winter, after the first growing season, select four, five, or six good scaffold branches positioned around the tree, spaced 4 to 5 inches apart on the trunk. Remove all other branches. Cut back the leader and the scaffolds by one-half to two-thirds their length.

During the next few years pruning will keep the tree small and induce spurs and flower buds close in on the branches. Remove sucker growth and crossing branches. The second winter, cut back new growth by a third. Keep the central leader stopped at 4 or 5 feet. The pear often produces more terminal shoot growth and may require more severe cutting back.

Peaches, Cherries, and Plums

Peaches on a dwarfing rootstock are commonly received as one-year-old whips that should be headed low (18 to 24 inches) and trained with three to five scaffold branches. The first winter, cut back new growth by one-third to one-half and then keep strong branches limited by cutting back and shaping the tree. Because a peach tree grows faster, it needs more severe pruning than an apple or pear tree.

Sour cherries usually have several laterals. Only four or five should be retained, the lowest about 1½ feet above ground. Cut back the central leader to 40 inches and the laterals to one-half their length; only light pruning is needed thereafter. Sweet cherries, on the other hand, are inclined to grow erect, so head back the leader at 5 or 6 feet and select four, five or six branches properly spaced for scaffold branches. Cut the new growth one-half the first winter, and thereafter keep the head thinned and shaped.

Japanese plums are handled like peaches, but 'Damson' is treated like sweet cherry; European plums are between the two. You must keep plums thinned out. Do not head back the terminals as this induces thick growth.

This tree was allowed one year's growth after planting, and then pruned as shown. "Low" pruning makes for easy picking from the mature tree.

5 ESPALIERS

The art of espalier originated in France and Italy about 400 years ago. An espalier tree is essentially one that has been trained to grow flat, in two dimensions instead of three. The tree is usually supported by a framework or a wall although free-standing espaliers are sometimes grown. Espaliers save space, and since they can be trained against masonry walls that absorb heat and radiate it back to the plants, various kinds and varieties of fruit that are not quite hardy enough to produce in the open can be grown.

An espalier is also an extremely ornamental way to display fruiting and flowering plants and a beautiful solution to the problem of the bare walls and fences so common in contemporary architecture. In the modern garden, the opportunity to save space and to develop a large expanse of color in a sliver of soil between the sidewalk and a wall has become important. You can creat the illusion of a great mass of plant material by this skillful use of just two dimensions.

Free-standing forms are usually one of three shapes: pyramidal; roughly triangular with the largest dimension at the base; or columnar with the branches of equal width at top and bottom. The trees are kept pruned in proportion to their height to expose a maximum of leaf surface to the sun, encouraging flower and fruit production. The more popular and practical supported forms have three basic types: cordons, palmettes, and informal designs.

Espaliers are handsome as background plants. Here dwarf fruit trees have been trained against a fence wall.

CORDONS

The simplest supported forms are the cordons (literally "string"); they may be vertical, horizontal, or oblique. These forms are excellent for the spur fruits. The non-spur, tip-bearing varieties of apples, 'Permain,' and 'Cortland,' should be avoided. Pears and plums also adapt to this method; peaches and nectarines do not. Because cordons can be spaced 1 or 2 feet apart and placed along a walk where the necessary pruning can be done easily, the cordon is an excellent technique for the home gardener.

Cordon variations include the double vertical, or U-forms, with arms 15 inches apart, and the serpentine, where the branches are curved into a series of reverse S's for a more decorative effect. This latter form helps to maintain a low height on especially vigorous varieties, and the bending tends to hasten fruiting.

The oblique cordon may be single or double, and if the branches overlap those of the neighboring trees the form is called a "Belgian fence." This makes a screen that separates parts of the garden.

Horizontal cordons may be trained with two or more tiers of branches. The most closed form is the arched cordon, or arcure; a series of whips without side shoots are planted 3 feet apart and slanted in one direction. When the tree is about 48 inches tall it is arched over and fastened near the base of the next tree. Near the top of the arch a single vertical shoot is allowed to grow, and when it is 4 feet long, it is arched in the reverse direction and fastened to the adjacent tree. This procedure may be continued to form a tier of arches to any height.

Training Cordons

The easiest espalier system is the horizontal cordon. Begin with an unbranched whip (called a maiden), and plant it 6 to 12 inches from the wall or trellis. Cut off the top at the height you want the first cordon to form — this may be from 12 to 20 inches above ground. When new shoots appear, retain only two for a single cordon, but leave the center one to grow vertically. When the leader reaches the desired height, cut it off to form the new shoots. Select two shoots, unless you want a third tier, in which case select three shoots. You may continue if more tiers are desired.

Start the vertical, or U-shaped, cordon the same as the horizontal, but when the branches attain 10 or 12 inches, bend them upward and tie them to lath or bamboo strips constructed vertically. Usually 16 inches is the proper spacing for vertical branches. Form double and triple U-forms by cutting the vertical branch at the height the U-s are wanted and selecting two strong branches to grow horizontally. They can be turned then to the vertical position.

Begin the Belgian fence by planting whips against a fence or frame, spacing them 2 feet apart. To make an effective pattern use a minimum of five whips cut at 18 inches, and when new shoots appear, select two and train them at opposite 45° angles.

By allowing each oblique branch to form two or more laterals, a lozenge design that can carry the diamond pattern higher than the simpler Belgian fence methods is created. Trees can be spaced farther apart, but always allow enough room so that there is ample open space between the branches bearing the fruit spurs.

For extremely vigorous varieties in an area where the growing season is long, the gridiron pattern may

be possible. This consists of a balanced pair of horizontal branches with six vertical branches 16 inches apart. Allow them to grow three on each side of the trunk, parallel to each other. If horizontals are trained from each vertical, a huge design is possible.

You can achieve the graceful arcure system by planting whips at an angle, leaning to the right three feet apart. After they are established, bend the tip of each whip to form a half-circle, and tie them. As shoots burst along the length of the curved stem, reserve one in the center, and when the shoot attains sufficient size, bend it over in the opposite direction and tie the tip into the base of the shoot, making the curve to the left. This procedure may be repeated as many times as necessary to achieve the desired height, because a branch bent with its tip low will not increase in length.

The Bouche-Thomas method of creating an arcure design is used to a limited extent in France and relies almost exclusively on bending, slanting, and weaving of the branches instead of cutting. The method utilizes the principle that vertical branches promote growth while oblique or arched branches promote fruitfulness. The whips are set in pairs at an acute angle, slanting toward each other to form an X, and tied where they intersect. The second year they are induced to form shoots near the base and toward the tip. These shoots grow erect until they are long enough to be bent backward and pegged to the ground. The third year, strong shoots from the base of the adjacent trees are crossed and tied where they intersect.

Henri Lepage of Angers, Belgium developed another alternative about 1925. In this method, young apple trees are planted 4 to 7 feet apart and, in commercial orchards, in 10-feet wide rows. On a trellis of three wires (the lowest 1½ feet above ground), the trees are bent and tied to the lowest wire in an arched position. At the top of the bend a strong shoot is induced, and next year this sprout is bowed and arched in the opposite direction and tied to the second wire. The third year, a similarly

Double horizontal cordon

Arcure technique

Belgian fence

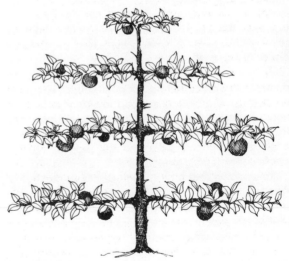

Horizontal T

placed shoot is tied to the third wire. With very vigorous varieties, a fourth tier can be added. The bending and tying is done as simply as possible. This gives the system wide appeal. 'Delicious' is not suited to this method, as the wood snaps when bent.

Summer Pruning of Cordons

Cordons must be pruned in the summer, and the Lorette system (after Louis Lorette, a professor at a small agricultural school in Wagnonville, France) is ideally suited for garden use in the latitude of northern France, where summer days are extra long. But because *all* the pruning is done during the summer months, when being in the garden is most enjoyable, the method appeals to all home gardeners.

In the early spring, when the new growth of laterals is about 2 inches long, cut the terminal growth back into last season's growth. Remove about one-fourth of last season's growth if the branches are vigorous, but if they are less vigorous cut them back one-half to check terminal growth and to stimulate adventitious buds on the stub that develops fruit buds. All laterals 4 inches apart should be removed completely except fruiting laterals (spurs). Allow the erect stem to grow undisturbed; make small cuts to maintain balance. Cut back the laterals sharply when they attain 12 inches and are about the diameter of a pencil. They will be about half woody. Fruiting spurs develop from these stubs.

Toward the end of July for pears and the last of August for apples, all 12-inch shoots should be cut back again to about ⅜ inch. A month later the rest of the shoots that are a foot in length should be treated in the same way. Any vegetative shoots that form on the stub should be bent downward and pierced or slit to stimulate the formation of fruit buds.

Trees must be kept vigorous; a deep, well-drained soil with good texture and high fertility is necessary. This method is best where there is little winter injury and where summers are not excessively hot. The number of flowers developed by the Lorette method is almost unbelievable: 30 inches of branch may carry a hundred flower clusters, each with as many as thirteen blossoms. Thus the tree must be drastically thinned, as a spacing of 3 inches apart is considered the minimum for fruit.

In a modified Lorette technique, as practiced in Europe, all mature laterals are cut back to three leaves in mid-June or early July; any secondary shoots are cut back to a single leaf. This cutting is done after the first flush of leaves mature. At this time the lower half of the stem is woody and about the thickness of a lead pencil. Immature shoots are passed over. In September, these shoots and any others that have developed (but *not* the leader) are cut back similarly. There are some indications that adhering strictly to this method, although it creates a beautifully controlled effect, reduces productivity. Also, this method is not well-adapted to our continental climate with its extremes of winter cold and summer heat and its variations in the amount of growth from year to year.

PALMETTES

The palmette espalier is shaped like the palm of the hand; the branches (fingers) radiate from a central point. Although considered the most elegant, this style was not developed because of its good looks alone: the bending of the branches prevents excessive vegetative growth and promotes fruiting and flowering.

The palmette form is achieved by allowing lateral branches to develop about 12 inches high on the trunk. Selected laterals that come off in pairs should be trained in opposite directions. There are horizontal, oblique, candelabra, and fan palmettes, but the most fascinating is the Verrier, considered the ultimate in grace and manageability.

Verrier Palmette

This form, promoted by Louis Verrier at Saulieu, France in 1849, is composed of a vertical axis from which regularly spaced lateral branches arise in pairs. (The presence of this central axis identifies the Verrier method.)

The arms are first trained almost horizontally and are then turned at the tips when the desired width has been attained. The arms at the lowest level are the widest, and with each tier the widths diminish. (See the illustration.) The number of arms is adjusted naturally to the vigor of the variety; the soil and climate also influence the shape.

Horizontal Palmette

This espalier consists of a single central trunk on which equally spaced, lateral branches are allowed to grow horizontally in pairs. The number of pairs depends on the fertility of the soil and other growing conditions, including the vigor of the trees. The branches may be of equal length or pyramid-shaped.

Oblique Palmette

This is similar to the horizontal except that the branches are trained at a desired angle. However, unless it is combined with alternating pyramidal-horizontal palmettes, much wasted space is left beneath the lowermost branches.

Verrier palmette

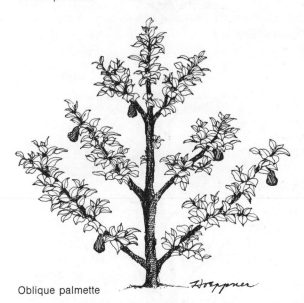

Oblique palmette

Informal fan shape

Free-form

Informal oblique palmette

Informal U-shape

INFORMAL ESPALIERS

Informal espaliers are well adapted to peaches and nectarines because a long annual shoot is necessary to produce fruit, and consequently, fruited wood must always be replaced. Peaches and nectarines are not suited to formal espaliers because it is impossible to limit their growth as rigidly as with the spur-type fruits and still get sufficient new wood to form fruit buds.

The best woods for the informal espalier are those with decorative bark. Do not use an intricate framework behind the informal espalier or you spoil the simple effect. Although this design does not need as much care as a formal pattern, it cannot be neglected for long; you should not allow trees to overgrow or grow wild. The greatest contribution to the beauty of an informal espalier display is the selection of a simple but elegant design. Choose a design that is suitable for the area to be covered. For example, a high wall should have a vertical accent; a low wall looks best with a horizontal line.

Methods for Informal Training

Training an informal espalier is a continuing job — it never ends as long as each season lasts. Much summer pinching is involved, and some daily time has to be spent with the plants to prevent ungainly growth habit. You can start with a one-year old whip or a partially or fully trained espalier. Usually strong yearling whips are used, and oblique planting (set at a 45° angle in relation to the ground) is preferred to vertical, because this induces most of the buds to break instead of only those on the upper half of the tree.

You should begin training a young plant at once. After a leader is selected and tied to the support, choose the laterals that are already growing and spaced properly to form the framework, if possible. If they are not satisfactory, cut all the laterals; this will encourage new shoots to grow. These shoots can grow unchecked, but all others should be tipped, and wild shoots, or suckers, should be removed. To stop growth and induce laterals and spur branches to form, bend the tips of the horizontal branches downward and tie them in place to prevent the spread of the hormone that inhibits lateral bud development and stops further elongation of the branch.

For the fan-shaped espalier, head the trunk 6 to 12 inches above the soil line and allow a number of strong shoots to grow. Tie these shoots to a frame in a more-or-less erect fashion. The fruit will be borne on these shoots the following year. Each year allow a few new shoots to grow, and remove the limbs that have fruited. It is difficult to achieve a neat, precise pattern because there is not a great deal of new yearly growth, but fruiting must be restricted to keep the tree in good growing condition and to ensure plenty of replacement wood.

SUPPORTS FOR ESPALIERS

Dwarf trees may be so heavy when loaded with fruit they may need the support of strong posts made of galvanized pipe or 4 x 4 redwood, cedar, or cypress. Stretch stout, 14-gauge, galvanized wire between the posts, and use heavy turnbuckles for tightening. When planting next to a wall, leave a 12-inch space for better air circulation. This space also facilitates pruning, tying, and spraying. If trees are very heavy with fruit, thin out some fruit to prevent damage to the tree.

In Europe, most trees are grown on brick and stone walls, some of which have been specially built for this purpose. Often both sides are used, but west walls are favored for pears and plums, south and east walls for apples, peaches, and cherries. North walls are reserved for currants and gooseberries. Cement block, especially that laid with the open ends out, is excellent. Brick can also be set in an open pattern to facilitate ventilation.

To attach a heavy-duty wire frame to a wall, use a 2¼-inch floor flange with a 6-inch galvanized nipple, threaded at both ends. For wire, use ³⁄₁₆-inch vinyl-coated tiller cable or 10-gauge copper wire. Loop the cable or wire over the nipple and fasten with a ³⁄₁₆-inch galvanized-wire roof clip. At the opposite end, use a 3-inch turnbuckle, hooked at one end, to pull the wire tight. Use ½-inch bamboo to hold vertical or oblique branches.

To attach supports to a masonry wall, set lead expansion shields or rawl plugs into the mortared joints between the brick or stone, and insert screw eyes. Holes may be made in mortar with a star drill with a carborundum tip; the hole should be small enough so that the shields fit snugly when tapped with a hammer.

For informal espaliers, copper or aluminum nails may be driven into a wooden wall and the branches attached with plastic tape or inconspicuous jute cord. For masonry walls, use an eye screw embedded in a lead expansion shield.

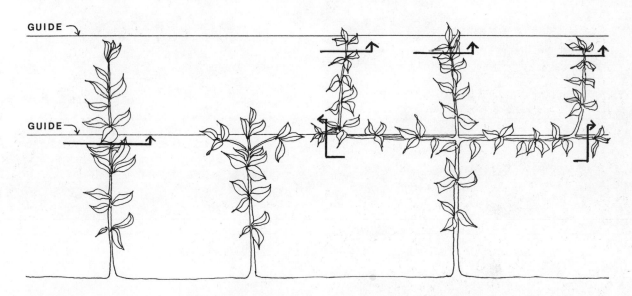

GUIDE

GUIDE

Prune to height of first joint

Train new shoots in desired direction

Keep pruning to keep new growth in espalier pattern

TRAINING ESPALIERS

ADRIÁN MARTÍNEZ

6 CARE OF MATURE TREES

Dwarf trees have shallower root systems than ordinary fruit trees and, consequently, need more attentive watering and fertilizing. It is time to water dwarf trees when the intervals between summer rains are long enough for lawns and garden flowers to require supplemental watering.

WATERING

Unless the trees are in a container, you cannot water them sufficiently with a hose. With the hose at full pressure it takes fifteen seconds to apply 1 inch of water to a large container. This much water can penetrate less than 12 inches in sandy soil, less than 4 inches in heavy loam. In the ground, roots cover a much wider area than when limited by a container, and water must be applied to the entire root-zone area.

A plant growing in the ground needs at least ten times more water than a container plant. Thus, where frequent summer watering is necessary, building a basin is recommended. The basin is used when the tree is planted and is useful as long as the tree grows. A basin should prevent runoff and utilize every drop of water you apply, and it should be made of earth with sides at least 4 inches high so that it can hold enough water to avoid many refillings.

Harvesting apricots from a dwarf tree in a mature orchard. (Photo: USDA)

When using sprinkler irrigation it is equally important to determine how long the sprinklers must run to supply adequate water to the roots. Determine this by setting 1-pound coffee cans at intervals adjacent to the sprinkler. Assuming that a 3-inch depth of water is needed to penetrate 3 feet of soil, measure the water in each can after fifteen minutes; you can then calculate the length of time the sprinklers have to be on to deliver that amount.

The amount of water you apply depends on the type of soil; the soil also affects the frequency of watering. Sandy soil must be watered every ten days, but a heavy soil in the same climate needs water only once a month. The frequency of watering is affected by the amount of rainfall and the rate of evaporation. In humid areas, lawns seldom need water after a month of drought; in the desert, where daily evaporation is 1 or 2 inches, this water loss must be replaced; dwarf trees might need watering every other day or twice a week. In most of the country, however, even in hot summer weather, established dwarf trees are not harmed by two weeks of drought, and two weeks between irrigations is ample.

Espaliered plants growing on the leeward side of a wall may be prevented from receiving beneficial rain that accompanies the prevailing wind. Trees planted under the eaves for frost protection will need much more watering than trees planted in the open.

MULCHING

A good mulch will reduce by at least 50 percent the amount of water lost by surface evaporation. Mulching also has other advantages. First, by keeping the soil surface moist it maintains cool temperatures in the warmest weather. This promotes root growth, for roots grow best in cool, moist soil, especially near the surface where the air content is highest; the soil in the upper 6 inches is usually the richest in the garden. Also, as organic mulches decompose, they add humus to the soil, making it more porous and aiding in water absorption.

Packaged mulches such as peat moss, manure, and shredded bark are available, but straw, grass clippings, chopped-up leaves, or compost will do equally well.

Pull the mulch a few inches away from the trunk, for soggy organic matter favors fungi and harbors mice and other rodents that may devour the bark. The high humidity mulch induces is also conducive to fungus attack.

If you want to grow a living mulch, such as a grass lawn or shallow-rooted ground cover, avoid weeds, long grasses, and deeply rooted ground covers. Grass sod is not compatible with tree roots because the necessary frequent watering demanded by lawns is usually too little and too frequent for trees. However, permanent holes, 1 or 2 inches in diameter, in the root zone will facilitate penetration of water and fertilizer. Fills the holes with gravel or well-rotted compost to keep them open.

Cultivation of your miniature orchard is not recommended. If you must control weeds with a hoe, cut them off at the surface, disturbing the soil as little as possible. You should use a thick mulch to control weeds, or one of the new weed control chemicals such as triflurilin (Treflan). Deeper cultivation is not necessary, and it may cause damage to the fine surface roots.

A 'Golden Delicious' dwarf apple, ten years old.
(Photo: USDA)

FERTILIZING

In addition to carbon, hydrogen, and oxygen in the air and water, a plant needs certain minerals found in the soil. The most important of these is nitrogen, the element needed to produce all protein. Phosphorous and potash are needed in relatively large quantities, but only tiny amounts of calcium, sulfur, iron, copper, zinc, manganese, and boron are necessary. The last 5 are commonly called "trace" elements. All but nitrogen are usually present in ample quantities in garden soil, but they may be bound up in soils whose reaction is too acid or too alkaline.

You can usually apply sufficient nitrogen to the soil by mulching with animal manure, but chicken manure must be composted before use, and it should be well mixed with straw or shavings. Since it is dangerous to apply too much nitrogen to fruit trees growing in average garden soil, it's best to use cattle or horse manure — they also supply potassium (potash) in sufficient amounts.

Most garden fertilizers are of the so-called balanced types, with nitrogen, phosphorous, and potash in standard amounts (a 6-10-4 formula has 6 percent nitrogen, 10 percent phosphorous, and 4 percent potash). In most soils little value is derived from the phosphorous in such a formula, and in certain instances it may do real harm; it may render the trace minerals unavailable by combining with them to form insoluble compounds.

Unless you have an orchard, and the low cost of the simple nitrogen compounds appeals to you, they should be avoided. Compounds such as urea (45 percent nitrogen), ammonium nitrate (33 percent nitrogen), and sulfate of ammonia (21 percent nitrogen), although cheap, make it very easy to apply too much. An overapplication may induce fertilizer burn: the margins of the leaves die, or in severe instances the entire tree dies. Trees that are given too much nitrogen also are more susceptible to winter injury and winter killing, and too much nitrogen can induce excessive vegetative growth and prevent

Well-grown 'Meyer' lemon in a stone planter. (Photo: Paul J. Peart)

flowering and fruit production. Finally, nitrogen fertilizers predispose apples and pears to fire blight.

Very poor soils may require two applications of fertilizers divided into equal amounts. (This is especially true on light soils.) The best fertilizers are organic, such as blood meal, tankage, cottonseed meal, fish meal, and other natural materials. The controlled-solubility compounds such as urea formaldehyde and the inorganic Mag Amp and coated fertilizers are also safe. Apply fertilizers containing ammonia in the fall. All organics require time to penetrate throughout the soil. Nitrate fertilizers like sodium and calcium nitrate are immediately available and may be applied very early in the spring; when fertilizer is applied regularly the application can be made at any time.

The greatest amount of nitrate that should be applied to core fruits is 1 ounce of high-analysis fertilizer per square yard. You may increase to ¼ pound blood meal and urea formaldehyde and ½ pound of cottonseed or fish meal. Stone fruits can be given 1 pound. If your trees are growing satisfactorily and yielding good crops, eliminate fertilizing entirely; they'll survive.

FOLIAR FEEDING

In an emergency, get quick results by applying nitrogen, phosphorous, potassium, and the trace minerals in a spray. These materials are quickly absorbed by the leaves and may correct deficiency symptoms overnight. Urea supplies nitrogen, orthophosphoric acid supplies phosphate, and potassium sulfate supplies potash. The sulfates of magnesium, iron, manganese, zinc, and copper supply these elements when applied directly to the leaves. Borax will correct a lack of boron when it is applied to the soil or leaves.

In 1916 it was discovered that results were better when citric acid was added to the sprays (before

A healthy dwarf cherry, used as a landscape tree.

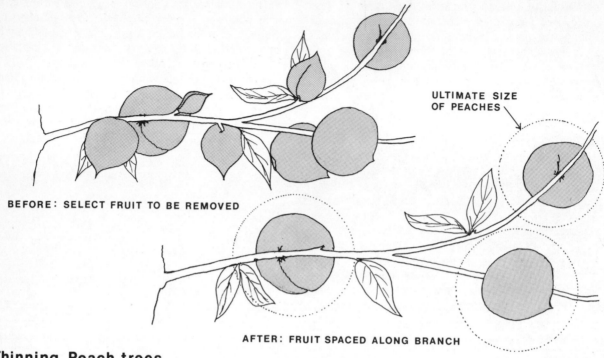

ULTIMATE SIZE
OF PEACHES

BEFORE: SELECT FRUIT TO BE REMOVED

AFTER: FRUIT SPACED ALONG BRANCH

Thinning Peach trees

application) containing metal sulfates because (as discovered later) plants absorb and utilize metals when these metals are combined with organic acids. Thus the widespread use of chelates (pronounced "key-lates") evolved. Chelates are organic compounds of iron, zinc, etc. that are more effective than inorganic compounds.

FRUIT THINNING

Thin fruits when they are the size of marbles. The time when this should be done will vary, of course, with the kind and the variety. Thinning prevents breakage of overloaded limbs and improves the size and quality of the fruit. Some plants, such as pears and cherries, rarely need thinning.

Peaches, apples, and nectarines should be about 6 inches apart, apricots about 3 inches. Peaches and nectarines are produced evenly along the branch, and it is easy to space them 6 inches apart, but for small-fruited varieties this space is too much. For larger fruits, such as the 'Hale' peach, 8-inch spacing is better.

Apples, plums, and apricots are produced on spur branches in clusters. One or two fruits per spur is not too many, or, if the set is uniformly heavy, one fruit on every two or three spurs will give a good crop. Spacing between fruits should be 2 to 4 inches.

When in doubt it is best to delay thinning; too early thinning may increase the amount of splitting and the number of gummy fruit. It is also more difficult to detect the culls early in the season. A number may fall during normal June drop.

Hand thinning should be done early; the earlier it is done the more benefits accrue. If you wait until the tree is in danger of breaking you may save the tree, but fruit size will not improve. Do not worry about taking off too much; some trees must have about 75 percent of their fruit removed in order to produce well.

The best tool for thinning large dwarf trees is a long pole with a piece of pliable hose attached to the end. With the pole it is possible to knock off the small fruits without injuring those left on the tree and damaging the tender leaves and bark.

When thinning apple and pear trees, keep in mind their tendency to alternate cropping. When they set a heavy fruit crop, they may fail to bloom and fruit the following year. This habit may endure year after year and is often accentuated in dwarf trees.

WIRE BRACING

When crops are heavy, limbs must be propped to keep them from breaking. Lumber can be used, but it is expensive to buy and bulky to store. Props must be removed for easy watering and maintenance after the crop is in.

If the taller dwarf trees bear heavily, try a better method of bracing: use center wiring. This method is inexpensive, long-lasting, and can be done at any time. The strain on one branch is supported by all the limbs, and during windstorms, breakage is less likely. However, the lack of ground obstruction is the biggest advantage.

Wire a tree after the tree has been pruned, unnecessary limbs have been removed, and foliage is out of the way. Wire braces often last for the life of the tree. Wiring is simple, for all you need are two ladders, a hammer, and wirecutting pliers. Use 1¼-inch fence staples (as many as the limbs you want to brace), 40 to 50 feet of 14-gauge galvanized wire, and one ⅝- or ¾-inch washer. Drive staples into the branches at a height just above the point where the limbs would break from heavy crops (10 to 12 feet above the ground in a mature tree). Slant the staples slightly off the line of the grain of the wood, but never across the grain. Drive the staple down until just enough space remains under the head to slip the wire through.

Hold the ring washer in the center of the tree, run a short length of wire to the nearest branch, and fasten it. Now connect an opposite branch to the washer with the staple wire, and continue this operation around the tree. Leave enough wire for slack, if necessary.

If lower, outside limbs need support, drive a staple on the lower side of an upper limb, opposite the wire support connection, and wire the lower branch to the upper. You can use a smaller staple for small branches. Except when the trees are bearing fruit, the wires should remain slack.

PRUNING

Mature dwarf fruit trees need little pruning. All pruning operations can be classified as trimming, heading back, and thinning out. Trimming is the light shaping of a tree; weak twigs and tips of branches are removed. When deeper cuts are advisable, such pruning is called heading back. Removal of an entire limb or part of a main limb down to a lateral branch is called thinning out.

These different methods have profound consequences. Whenever a terminal bud or "leader" is removed, the buds immediately below are stimulated into growth that may be desirable or undesirable, depending on what is wanted. When a branch is thinned out, the topmost lateral branch becomes the leader, and there is no stimulation of side branches. Heading back tends to thicken the top and make a denser tree; thinning out tends to make the top more open and allows easier access for spraying and picking operations.

The two cardinal principles of pruning are: always use sharp shears, and never try to cut too large a branch. Hand shears can cut a limb up to ¾ inch in diameter; lopping shears can cut a branch 1 inch thick. Any larger branches need a sharp saw. Sharp tools make clean cuts that heal quickly; dull tools mangle the living tissues and encourage fungi and bacteria.

First remove diseased, dead, broken, or crossing branches. Take out water sprouts (strong vertical shoots) and all suckers from the roots or base of the tree below the graft. Keep a constant watch, for dwarfing rootstocks sucker more than the normal rootstock. Remove these shoots while they are small and can be rubbed off. If you must cut them, be sure to remove all the stub. Keep the center of the tree open by heading back to an outside bud; when you thin out, cut to an outside branch.

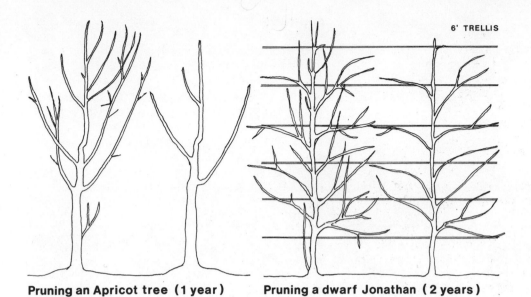

Pruning an Apricot tree (1 year)

Pruning a dwarf Jonathan (2 years)

6' TRELLIS

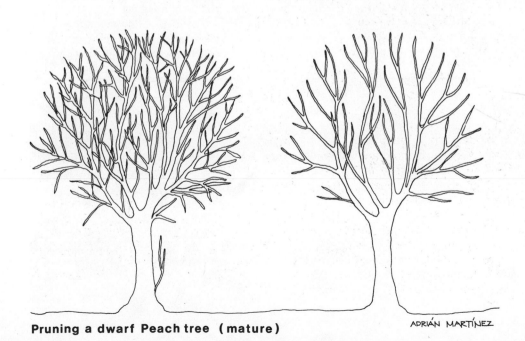

Pruning a dwarf Peach tree (mature)

ADRIÁN MARTÍNEZ

Apples and Pears

Bearing dwarf apple and pear trees need little pruning, but for semidwarf sizes, keep a balance between fruiting and vegetative growth. (The ideal is about 6 inches of new growth per year.) Too severe pruning can cause light crops and a large amount of non-fruiting growth. When pears set an excessive number of spur branches, some of these should be removed.

Cherries and Plums

Cherry and plum trees need little pruning. Just remove crossing and rubbing branches, and thin out branches to make the inside light and airy. More dead and damaged branches occur in cherry and plum trees than in apples and pear trees; these branches should be removed yearly. Plums have a greater tendency to get too thick and may need more thinning out.

Peaches and Nectarines

Peaches and nectarines require heavier pruning because their flowers and fruit are all produced on year-old wood. If little new wood is formed, the next year's crop may be limited. As dwarf fruit trees get older, new growth may be only a few inches at the tips of branches, and the fruit may be produced only at the ends of long leggy branches. By cutting back new growth by half each year, the form and production can be maintained.

'Bonanza' peach dominates a terrace corner. (Photo: Clint Bryant)

H.D

7 DISEASE AND PEST CONTROL

Home gardeners generally use small hand-powered equipment to apply sprays and dusts; bucket pumps, hose-end applicators, compressed air tanks, and trombone types are all satisfactory. You should have an adjustable nozzle that allows you to reach the tops of the semidwarf trees. For dusting, use the equipment in which the dusts are sold. Apply uniformly, but lightly. Heavy, visible deposits of dusts may injure some plants, and they are unnecessarily expensive. For satisfactory results, you must closely follow the timing schedule.

PHYSIOLOGICAL DISEASES

Young fruit trees are subject to sunburn, which is different from winter injury previously mentioned. To prevent sunburn, protect trunks with wrappers or a special paint.

Some of the most serious diseases of dwarf fruit trees (and the ones most easily remedied) are caused by mineral deficiencies. Generally, these minerals are not lacking in the soil, but the elements may be bound by adverse acidity or alkalinity and so are not available to plants.

Although light-green foliage may be a varietal characteristic, it is often caused by a lack of nitrogen. Conversely, dark-green leaves often indicate too much nitrogen; when this is the case, there will be excessive vegetative growth and diminished flowering and fruiting. A yellowing between the veins may result from an iron or manganese deficiency.

Deciduous fruit trees often have tufts or rosettes of yellow leaves that develop into "witches brooms" at the tips of the shoots. All these symptoms are alleviated with a spray of iron, manganese, or zinc chelates, or all may be combined in one spray. The best diagnosis is to apply the chelates and note the reaction. Sprayed nitrogen also can be applied to the leaves.

Boron deficiency in apples and pears causes russetting and cracking, with brown corky areas in the flesh of the fruit, especially near the calyx end. Correct by spraying the leaves with a solution of 2 pounds borax to 100 gallons of water (3 ounces to 10 gallons) or by scattering 2 ounces of boric acid in the soil under the tree. Too much boron causes equally serious damage, so do not use it unless the county agent or another authority recommends it.

Dwarf 'Ponderosa' lemon

Fire blight, a bacterial disease, has attacked this pear tree. Note the cankered trunk. (Photo: USDA)

Above, peaches infected with brown rot. Below, peaches with Rhizopus rot, another fungus disease. (Photo: USDA)

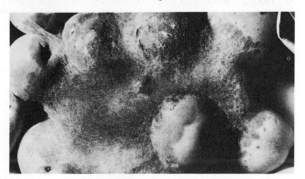

VIRUS DISEASES

Because fruit trees are propagated vegetatively (instead of with seeds), they are often riddled with an assortment of viruses that are almost impossible to kill. To control most virus diseases, insist on virus-free stock when you buy your plants.

There are two types of virus diseases: those that spread only when infected wood is budded or grafted and those that pass from tree to tree. The first disease can be eliminated by a certification program. Natural spread can be kept under control by starting clean trees, unless there is a source of nearby contamination. (Commercial growers have noted that there is virtually no spread from orchard to orchard.)

Some of the most serious virus diseases include stubby twig and mule's ear (they affect peaches and can be controlled by buying certified stock), pear decline, apricot ringspot, peach mosaic, and western X (which attacks all stone fruits except apricot and is spread by wild chokecherry). Citrus viruses include quick decline, excortis, and psorosis. 'Meyer' lemon is uniformly infected with quick decline of citrus (also called tristeza). Destroying badly damaged plants to prevent spread to healthy stock is recommended for the control of some viruses.

BACTERIAL DISEASES

Fire blight, crown gall, and canker or gummosis of stone fruits are the principal bacterial diseases. Pears, especially 'Bartlett,' are the most susceptible to fire blight. Apples and quinces and several other closely related ornamentals, including pyracanthas, loquats, mountain ashes, cotoneasters, and hawthorns are also affected by fire blight. Blackening of blossom clusters, death of tender young twigs, and cankers on the large branches and trunk indicate this disease.

Formerly, a spray of weak Bordeaux mixture (½:½:50) was recommended at full bloom, but now Agrimycin (used according to directions on package) is successful. It will control the blossom blight but not the cankers. Cankers must be pruned out.

Crown gall and the related disease hairy root are not easily controlled but can be eliminated from the rootstock if grown on sterilized soil. Crown gall is an overgrowth at base of plant and on roots. Gummosis may be caused by bacteria, insects, growth cracks, or fungus. A sticky resin exudes from stems, twigs, and trunk. Bacterial disease is best controlled by cutting out the blighted limbs and the diseased bark and burning the infected branches.

FUNGUS DISEASES

The most serious apple disease throughout the world is apple scab, a fungus that damages leaves, fruit, and twigs. The scab of pears, hawthorns, and mountain ashes cannot infect apples. There are areas where scab is unknown and other places where it rarely occurs. In some localities, scab may damage trees only one year in five, but in most apple-growing areas that are humid, scab-free years are infrequent.

Apple scab causes early leaf drop. If the disease appears, you will see circular flecks that show distinct branches, much like those of a tree. Sometimes the spots coalesce into a general browning of the leaves, often with distortion and curling. Lesions on the fruit are small, raised spots that soon break the skin and develop a rough, corky surface. Lesions similar to those on the fruit sometimes form on year-old twigs.

Repeated sprayings with captan, dodine (Cyprex), or lime sulfur effect control, or you may dust with sulfur. A spray program for apples is given in the Appendix table 10. (This table also lists programs for pears, cherries, peaches, nectarines, prunes, plums, and citrus.)

Powdery mildew is a disease that commonly affects young trees. This fungus can be controlled readily and thus should not be allowed to cause damage. It is controlled as a part of the regular spray program in the West, but elsewhere, an application of dinocap (Karathane) quickly cures the problem.

Apple rust first appears on the upper surface as pale-yellow spots that become orange-colored. Blisters on the under side of the leaf swell and rupture, producing clusters of cuplike structures. The rust fungus comes from red cedars (*Juniperus virginiana*) located nearby and can be controlled by eliminating this alternate host.

Brown rot causes the most damage to stone fruits, but it rarely affects pears and apples. Brown rot attacks and kills the blossoms, leaves, and twigs, produces cankers on the branches, and causes a fruit rot in the orchard and after harvest. It lives through the winter in mummified fruit and starts in the early spring by windblown spores. Collecting and destroying as much fallen fruit as possible is helpful, but dusting with sulfur or spraying with sulfur or Captan is recommended for more complete control. Recently, Botran has given good control of brown rot that develops in the field and after harvest.

Control leaf curl by applying a dormant spray to the falling autumn leaves. Bordeaux mixture formerly was the standard control measure, but good results with dodine (Cyprex) have been reported.

Shot hole is a fungus disease that attacks stone fruits and causes leaf spots which quickly fall out, leaving the foliage riddled as if it had been blasted with a shotgun. (The inexperienced often attribute the damage to insects.) This fungus also attacks twigs, producing long, brown cankers. This symptom, which results in the death of twigs, is called blight; the fungus responsible is a species of *Coryneum,* and can be controlled with dodine and

Captan. Shot-hole disease of cherries is caused by a different fungus, but it also can be controlled with dodine and Captan.

NEMATODES

Microscopic eelworms that attack roots damage plants grown in light soil in areas where the soil does not freeze deeply. Peaches and plums are very susceptible. Pears and quinces have some resistance, but apples, apricots, and some peach and plum rootstocks are highly resistant to the rootknot nematode. Citrus is highly susceptible to another kind called the citrus nematode.

For standard-sized trees, use the 'Nemaguard' rootstock for peaches and 'Mariana' for plums. However, for dwarf varieties, treat the soil with a chemical called dibromochloropropene (DBCP), sold under the trade names of Nemagon and Fumazone. It can be applied before planting to the hole or to established plants as a soil drench.

MITES

The advent and wide use of DDT to kill the predators of mites allowed these creatures to become a major pest. They attack all fruit trees and other crop plants and ornamentals, damaging chiefly in the warm, dry part of the year; in areas of heavy rainfall, mites are rarely a problem. They are not insects but belong to the spider family, having eight legs instead of six, and they cause damage with their rasping mouthparts. Some infect fruit and leaf buds and produce distortion. Sulfur in various forms was the standard control, but recently Omite and Kelthane have been used.

INSECTS

Aphids are soft-bodied insects with sucking mouthparts; the woolly apple aphid is covered with a woollike, waxy material. They reproduce rapidly and may cause severe damage before you realize an infestation has occurred. The damage is mostly curled or distorted leaves, and on evergreens such as citrus, the damaged leaves remain a disfiguring feature for several years. Aphids are easy to kill with insecticides; the best is probably diazinon (Spectracide). The rosy and the green apple aphids are limited to leaves, but the wooly apple aphid infests all parts of the tree, including the roots. They produce swollen and knotty galls on the twigs and roots, especially near wounds, and actively spread a canker caused by a fungus. Fortunately for dwarf-tree growers, the Malling-Merton apple rootstocks are resistant to this pest.

Thrips are tiny, rasping insects that attack many plants, including citrus. One type of thrip attacks the leaf and flower buds of apples, pears, and stone fruits.

The pear psyllids are about 1/10-inch long and fat-bodied: the adults have transparent wings held rooflike over their bodies. In addition to the damage they cause by chewing, psyllids produce a toxin that causes "psylla shock." Symptoms include yellow foliage, retarded growth, and poor fruit size and quality. They can be controlled by diazinon (Spectracide) used as a spray.

Sawflies are black, shiny insects resembling houseflies. They lay eggs that hatch into caterpillars or legless larvae (called slugs). The larvae feed voraciously on cherries, plums, quinces, and especially pears. They skeletonize the leaves, eating everything but the veins. Sevin is the best control.

Maggots are the larvae of true flies, and apple maggots feed on apples. European plums, and cherries. The maggot is considered the most important apple pest in the East. The adult, slightly smaller than a housefly, lays eggs in the fruit; the eggs hatch and tunnel in a winding route to the core. Sevin, applied when the flies appear (early June near New York City), gives control.

The coddling moth is a universal pest that causes wormy fruit. It attacks pears and quinces and occasionally apricots, cherries, peaches, and plums. A regular program of spraying with Sevin (properly timed and carefully applied), will give satisfactory control. The newest insecticide for controlling coddling moths, apple maggots, plum curculios, pear psyllids, and oriental fruit moths is Imidian, an organophosphate.

Beetles that damage fruit trees include curculios which sting and enter the fruit, the Japanese beetles whose larvae feeds on the roots, and the round and flat-head and shot-hole borers which infest the bark. Other borers are moth larvae, including the several peach-tree borers and the peach-twig borer. For control of Japanese beetles and the disease caused by them, Sevin seems to be effective. Control peach tree borers with applications of diazinon applied to the branches in a regular program. Insecticides that repel the beetles or kill the larvae have not consistently killed flat-head borers. Apply white paint to the trunk upward 1 inch below ground to prevent both sunburn and the infestations. Wrapping trunks with cardboard, newspaper, or tarpaper also reduces egg laying.

Leafhoppers are tiny green insects that jump and feed by sucking. They cause leaf damage and carry several virus diseases. They are easily controlled with diazinon.

Scale insects are many and varied, but all are armored or covered with the hard shell that gives them their name. Formerly, the only control was an oil applied to dormant trees in the wintertime, but with the new organophosphate insecticides better results have been obtained. Diazinon, mixed with oil, gives good results.

Scale, aphids, and psyllids produce honeydew, a sweetish secretion that attracts ants. Some fungi that grow readily in this sticky substance are called sooty molds. They can be wiped off the leaf, leaving the surface underneath green and unharmed. Control of the insects prevents accumulation of the honeydew and the growth of the fungi.

H.D.

8 HOW TO GROW YOUR OWN DWARF FRUIT TREES

Fruit varieties available from most nurseries have been developed to fill commercial needs for keeping-quality, good appearance, high-productivity, and ease in shipping. Tender-skinned fruit with soft, juicy flesh does not ship well; and when the plant breeder succeeds in producing a stone fruit with keeping quality it usually lacks juiciness and flavor as well. In short, orchard varieties must be profitable rather than tasty.

Few projects in gardening are more rewarding than creating your own dwarf orchard, for then all varieties are of your own choosing. You can have a succession of peaches ripening in the summer, and if you have space for only one tree, you can still have four or five varieties. If you are tired of a variety or have a tree that doesn't do well, you can change the entire tree to new varieties, or change only one branch at a time!

GROWING FROM SEED

You can grow your own seedlings from seed, and bud them as a nurseryman does. Seeds of most fruits grow easily, and you can bud them with any handy variety. However, the seeds will produce standard-size plants, and to get a dwarf rootstock, you will have to buy dwarf seed or propagate from a dwarf rootstock by one of several methods.

Seed can be purchased from seed importers and collectors who make a specialty of dwarf seeds. Large seeds of peaches, plums, apricots, and cherries can be planted outdoors in the fall, and they will germinate in the spring; but apples and quinces must be planted in a flat, and they must be kept cool and moist. When the seedlings emerge, transplant them to pots and move them to a sunny location. Potted seedlings 6 to 8 inches tall can be planted about a foot or two apart in rows. They can be budded where they are growing.

The most reliable means of getting dwarf rootstocks is by vegetative propagation, using one of the following methods.

Dwarf 'Kim' Elberta peach

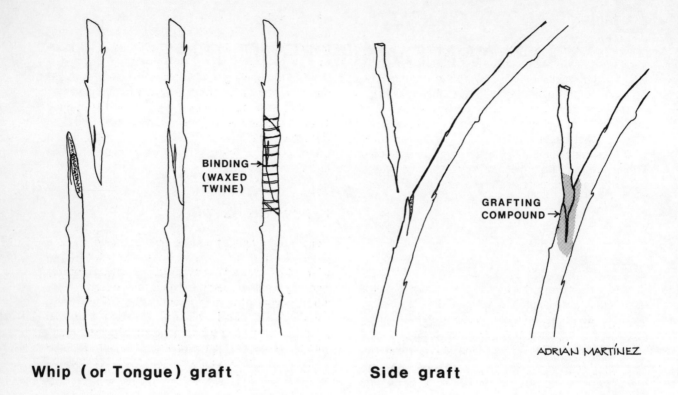

BINDING (WAXED TWINE)

GRAFTING COMPOUND →

ADRIÁN MARTÍNEZ

Whip (or Tongue) graft   **Side graft**

LAYERING

A dwarf rootstock that produces a shoot (sucker) may be grown horizontally and notched with a sterile knife (make a "V" cut) at the ground line. Bury the notch below the surface of the ground or, if it doesn't bend easily, put a mound of soil over the stem. This will induce buds to grow and form roots. To get several plants, bury an entire lower limb in a trench about 4 inches deep. Use staples of heavy wire to hold the branch down, and, as the shoots form, add more and more soil to the trench. The following year, you can cut the new plants away from the mother plant.

STOOLING

Another method is to mound soil over the base of a plant that is cut back to the soil line. Shoots emerge from the stump in the spring and form roots in the mound of soil. The shoots may be cut away and planted separately in the following dormant season. Some rootstocks, notably plum and cherry, are propagated by cutting away suckers that are formed naturally.

SOFTWOOD CUTTINGS

Fresh new growth on a plant is called "softwood." Anyone who has done much gardening has made softwood cuttings called "slips" which are pieces of stem with the leaves intact. When making cuttings you must reduce the number and size of the leaves, or the stem will dry out and die.

Cut a 4- to 5-inch stem, and remove the lower leaves. Cut the upper leaves in half to reduce transpiration. Place cuttings in a polyethylene sack half-full of moistened planter mix. (Pieces with two or three buds are preferable.) Cut off and discard the soft stem tip, and treat the base of the stem with a rooting hormone. Insert the cuttings an inch or more into the planter mix, and close the bag at the top. Set in a bright, warm (60° to 70°F) location.

All of the Malling apple rootstocks can be propagated by this slip method. Cherries and peaches will also respond. The best time to start is in June or July, unless the mother plants can be forced to produce suitable shoots by bringing them into a greenhouse. In that case, you can make cuttings in March.

HARDWOOD CUTTINGS

Collect the stems of mature dormant shoots 7 to 8 inches long, of the current season's growth (one-year old), in early November or before severe freezing weather begins. These are called "hardwood." Store at cool temperatures (40°F) in damp sand or peat moss, with the stems in a vertical position. Plant in the spring, 2 or 3 inches apart, with the upper bud just above the soil line. In mild-winter areas, fall planting is preferable. This method is especially good for obtaining quince rootstocks and some plums.

BUDDING

The most common method of propagating woody plants vegetatively is by budding. In this operation, a dormant bud of the desired variety is placed on the stem of the rootstock; after it becomes established it is stimulated into growth by cutting away the entire stem of the rootstock above the bud. This leaves the bud, also called the "eye," in the dominant topmost position, where it will produce the new plant. Budding must be done during the summer, when the rootstock is growing actively and before the bark has tightened. This time will vary, depending on the kind of fruit as well as on the latitude, climate, soil, and disease conditions. In the New York area, the following dates are generally good:

Pears	July 10 - 20
Apples	July 13 - September 1
EM IX	August 10 - September 1
'St. Julien' Plum	July 15 - August 1
Sand Cherry	August 1 - 10
Quinces	July 25 - August 15
Peaches	August 20 - September 10

How to Bud

Cut shoots of the desired variety to obtain the budwood. Cut off the leaves except for a short spur of leaf stem; this spur acts as a handle with which to lift the bud. Immediately after cutting, wrap the bud in damp burlap and never allow it to become dry. Use the center buds on the stick of budwood, never the tip bud or the bottom bud. Use plump but hard buds. The rootstock, whether obtained from seed or from a nursery, is budded just above the soil line (4 inches). After the bud is set, the entire plant above the point where the bud is inserted is cut off so that all growth is concentrated in the bud.

Place the bud 5 to 6 inches above the collar of the rootstock; if the desired variety is susceptible to collar rot, place the bud 12 inches above. At the point where the bud is to be inserted, make a T-shaped cut: first make the cross incision by rocking the knife back and forth; then make the vertical cut by drawing the knife upward from an inch below the cross cut. Cut only the bark. With a twist of the blade, loosen the corners of the bark so that they can be raised easily.

Start below the bud. Hold the knife horizontally and cut upward. Cut the entire thickness of the bark to provide a firm base for the bud and surrounding tissues (called the "bud shield"). Cut only a sliver of wood under the eye.

Lift the bud without tearing it, using the stem piece, and insert it into the T-shaped cut. Push down the base of the bud shield until the top is level with the transverse cut. The corners of the bark should envelop the shield, leaving the bud sticking out.

Next tie the bud shield firmly with rubber bands 2 inches long and 3/8 inch wide. Place a rubber band above the bud, and beginning at the bottom, wind the rubber tautly and smoothly upward, covering everything except the bud, or eye. In a few weeks, the still-dormant bud will have united with the rootstock, and the rubber bands may be severed.

The following spring, before growth has started, remove the top of the rootstock above the dormant bud. This forces the bud into rapid growth. However, it may also stimulate into growth other buds that must be removed before they are large enough to cause damage. Other buds arising from the rootstock will take over if allowed to grow and will smother the growth of the desired variety.

STEM GRAFTING

Scions of a desired variety, cut into 6-inch sections and grafted to the rooted portion of a rootstock, may be united by a "tongue" (whip) or "cleft" graft. Cut off the top of the rootstock with an upward, slanting cut about 1½ inches long and discard it. About ½ inch down the slanting surface, cut a vertical "tongue" or "cleft" parallel to the length of the rootstock. Cut the scion with the tongue or cleft cut out so that they can be dovetailed together with the growth tissue of each in contact, just under the bark. Wind tape or cloth around the union and keep it in a cool place until the spring, when the graft can be set out in the garden.

DOUBLE WORKING

If the scion and rootstock are incompatible, impose a stem piece between the two. This technique is also used in dwarfing. Sometimes, by double budding, (the rootstock is budded to the compatible variety; when it grows it forms a stem), a bud of the desired variety is inserted. This procedure takes three years to produce a one-year-old tree. The technique is used with apples and pears by whip grafting a stem piece with a scion of the desired variety grafted to it. The rootstock and the stem piece scion are then put together in the spring, when the rootstock is cut off several inches above the ground and the combination is made just as growth starts. This produces a tree in one season that attains the same height as one that is budded once.

H.D.

9 CLIMATE ADAPTATIONS AND VARIETIES

CORE FRUITS

Apples

Apple varieties may be classified as early, medium, and late, depending on ripening. The hardiest early varieties are 'Yellow Transparent,' 'Anoka,' and 'Oldenburg' ('Duchess'). Midseason varieties are 'Patten' or 'Greening,' 'Wealthy,' 'Grimes Golden,' and 'Wolf River.' Late varieties are 'McIntosh,' 'Cortland,' 'Jonathan,' 'Delicious,' 'Haralson,' and 'Northwestern Greening.' Some 'McIntosh' seedlings, including 'Red Melba,' 'Lobo,' 'Milton,' and 'Macoun,' are also satisfactory. All should be grafted on hardy rootstocks. In Canada, the 'Heyer 12' is considered the hardiest commercial apple.

Subtropical areas present the equally grave problem of lack of winter chilling. 'Beverly Hills,' 'White Pearmain,' and 'Winter Banana' are best-adapted in these areas. An apple discovered in Queensland, Australia, called 'Tropical Beauty,' has borne fruit in Hawaii and southern Florida. It needs no pollination to set fruit, but the apples are often seedless.

In the huge geographical area between southern Florida and northern Canada there are many favorite varieties; over 5,000 have been named. The best-known older variety is the 'McIntosh,' which was found by John McIntosh when he was clearing some land in Dundas County, Ontario, Canada, about the time of the American Revolution. It is a seedling of the snow apple, an old French variety named 'Fameuse.' In the warmest areas it will drop its fruit when ripe, a serious fault in a commercial orchard. A well-known seedling of McIntosh is 'Cortland'; it was developed by the Geneva Experiment Station in New York and is obtained from a 'McIntosh' 'Ben Davis' cross.

The best-known newer variety is 'Golden Delicious,' discovered in 1914 in West Virginia. The original tree still stands near the town of Queen Shoals, at the Mullens Farm. It was enclosed in a steel cage with a burglar alarm when it was purchased for $5,000 in 1917. Thousands of grafts of this tree have been made and planted throughout the temperate zone, but the original tree still bears its fruit under the care of the county agricultural agent. The parentage of this seedling is not known. Some believe its parents were the 'Golden Reinette,' a popular European variety, and 'Grimes Golden,'' the pollen parent. If this is true it is related to the original 'Delicious' in name only.

Dwarf bing cherry

The most popular apple variety, the 'Delicious,' was found growing as a seedling in Iowa. It was planted in 1872, and the probable parentage was a 'Winesap' pollinated by 'Yellow Bellflower.' In 1893, in a contest for new apple varieties, Jesse Hiatt of Winterset sent in the fruit. He called the apple 'Hawkeye,' but when Stark Brothers bought the tree they named it 'Delicious.' The characteristic long, tapering shape and the five prominent knobs at the blossom end make this apple easily identifiable.

'Jonathan' is an all-purpose apple found in upper New York State. It was introduced by Jonathan Hasbrouck, for whom it was named. It is thought to be a seedling of 'Spitzenberg.' The tart flavor and good storage ability make this an all-around favorite for cooking and eating; it is the best variety to use when making apple butter.

In the Winesap family, the 'Stayman Winesap' variety, generally conceded to be the best-flavored apple, has superseded the original. It was grown in a crop of 'Winesap' seed planted by Dr. J. Stayman in Kansas during the War Between the States. Like the 'Winesap,' the 'Yellow Newtown' traces its ancestry back to Colonial times.

'Rome Beauty,' generally considered best for baking, is an old variety that originated in Ohio. It often fails to color up well and thus has been superseded by a red sport, 'Red Rome.'

The most famous yellow apple before 'Golden Delicious' was the 'Grimes Golden.' It originated at Fowlersville, West Virginia. Legend says that it came from a seed sown by Johnny Appleseed, who was Jonathan Chapman, an itinerant preacher. He wandered up and down the Ohio Valley between 1806 and 1847 reading religious tracts to settlers and Indians and planting apple seeds. The variety was discovered and named by Thomas Grimes in 1832. The tree blew down in 1900, and now two stone pillars and a watering trough mark the spot where it stood.

An oldster who yearns for his lost boyhood often has a nostalgic yearning for a 'Duchess' Baldwin ('Duchess of Oldenburg' is its full name), 'Northern Spy,' or a 'Fameuse.' He is certain that these old varieties had more character, sprightliness, and flavor than the glamorous beauties sold in the supermarkets. To savor the flavor of these lost varieties, visit the Old Variety Orchard planted by the Worcester County Horticultural Society on the S. Lathrop Davenport Farm at North Grafton, Massachusetts.

'Duchess of Oldenburg' is of Russian origin and came to America via England in 1835. It is a good cooking apple, excellent for pies and sauce. 'Baldwin' came from a seedling found on the farm of John Ball at Wilmington, Massachusetts about 1740. During the Civil War it was the most popular variety in New England.

The old apple variety 'Northern Spy' originated on the farm of Herman Chapin near Rochester, New York. It takes a long time to come into bearing, but dwarfs on Malling rootstocks have solved this problem. The 'Fameuse,' also called the 'Snow Apple' because of its white flesh, was brought into the Midwest by the early French missionaries before 1700. (Apple varieties and their fruit characteristics are listed in Appendix table 2.)

Crab Apples

Crab apple trees are generally small (usually less than 20 feet tall), and some are the size of shrubs. Apple trees with fruit less than 2 inches in diameter are classified as crab apples; they may be seedlings or cultivated varieties. Most varieties now sold are crosses between the Siberian species *Malus baccata* and standard varieties, but they are generally called Siberian crabs. Their great hardiness enables them to grow in the coldest parts of this country and Canada.

Pears

These are ancient fruits; judging from the accounts of the pre-Christian Greeks and Romans the fruit has been vastly improved. Although there were over 40 varieties known to the ancient world, Pliny said that they should be boiled or baked with honey to become "wholesome to the stomach."

There were 250 varieties known in Europe when the colonies were settled. In the eighteenth century, a priest of Mons, Belgium, developed the first types; they had soft, melting flesh. Later a Belgian physician raised more than 80,000 seedlings from which he selected 40 superior kinds.

Pears are more limited in their climate requirements than apples; they are not as hardy in cold winters, and they need more winter chilling. Therefore, they are best adapted to zones 5 io 8. The quality of pears is improved by cool weather, and they gain in flavor, color, and keeping quality when grown at higher altitudes. The pear is better-adapted to withstanding hot weather than the apple. However, some pear varieties are susceptible to fire blight, an endemic bacterial disease of pears, so select carefully. Shortly after 1770, this dread disease ravaged new pear plantings. It has been a limiting factor in the growth of pears ever since.

The sand pear, a species (Pyrus pyrifolia) introduced from Japan before 1840, is resistant to fire blight, and natural crosses resulted in the selection of the 'Kieffer' variety in 1873. Although improved blight-resistant varieties that are better-tasting than the 'Kieffer' have continued to appear, they do not yet compare with the Bartlett in quality. The sand pears have stone cells or grit interspersed in the fruit, but many nurseries still stock the 'Kieffer.' It has the widest climate range of any pear variety, adapting to the deep South and to the rugged winters of zone 4.

The 'Tyson and the 'Seckel' are native American varieties that appeared near Philadelphia during the Revolution. 'Seckel' is the best garden variety because of its vigor, productivity, and resistance to blight. The fruit, though small and unattractive, is of high quality. The flesh is sweet and spicy. The 'Tyson' is sometimes called the 'Summer Seckel' because it ripens earlier, with melting flesh and honeyed flavor. It is also blight-resistant.

Other blight-resistant varieties are 'Moonglow' and 'Magness.' Developed by the U.S. Department of Agriculture, both have good quality. Another pear similar to 'Bartlett' in flavor and appearance is the 'Stewart Bartlett,' developed in the Northwest.

All other pear varieties are measured by the 'Bartlett.' It dominates the commercial market, and while it is available, from July to October, other varieties are at a distinct disadvantage. Some gourmets look down on this variety, but most people regard it highly. 'Bartlett' was named after Enoch Bartlett of Massachusetts. He imported the variety from England, where it was supposedly raised as a seedling by a man named Williams under whose name it is known there. However, it is similar, if not identical, to the 'Bon Chretien,' an ancient French pear.

Although 'Bartlett' pears may attain a weight of 27 ounces and a girth of 13 inches, the 'Pound' variety is the largest, with enormous fruits weighing to 5 pounds. 'Comice' (full name 'Doyenne du Comice'), grown chiefly for gifts ('Royal Riviera'), is the largest commercial variety. The biggest fruits for the home garden are those of 'Duchess,' whose full name is 'Duchesse d'Angoulême.'

The most cold-resistant variety is 'Clapp Favorite,' but it is highly susceptible to fire blight. 'Stark Krimson' is a sport with red fruit. The fruit resembles 'Bartlett' but does not have the musky taste.

The 'Gorham' pear variety was developed at the New York Experiment Station by crossing the Bartlett with a sweet, pink-fleshed little pear called 'Josephine de Malines.' 'Gorham' is yellow with white, juicy flesh and musky flavor. A sport of 'Gorham,' grandiloquently named 'Grand Champion,' is very popular in Europe, where it is perfect for eating "out of hand."

The 'Bosc' ('*Beurré Bosc*'), with a long tapering stem end, was developed in Belgium. It bears in September and is a good keeper. (Pear varieties and fruit size are listed in Appendix table 3.)

Quinces

Quinces, more adaptable to various climates than any other fruit, are scarce in the home garden, perhaps because they are not commercially popular. But the trees, which seldom grow higher than 8 to 12 feet, are well-suited to the modern garden, and the fruit is flavorsome if made into sauce or jelly. Characteristically, the large, applelike fruit, often weighing 1 pound each, are covered with felt-like fuzz. The trees bloom late and generally are not affected by frost. Quinces survive the cold better than pears but do not do well in hot zones.

STONE FRUITS

Plums

There are many different kinds of plums, with a great diversity of climate adaptation, size, taste, color, and form. Most cultivated kinds are good for eating. The fresh and wild sorts are tart enough to make excellent jelly. The small trees bear heavily and are well suited to small yards and gardens. From the crosses between the sand cherry and large plum varieties, low-bush types have been created that withstand the northermost environment. These are 'Sapa,' 'Opata,' 'Compass,' 'Manor,' and 'Dura.' They produce heavy crops of rich, sweet fruits and are self-pollinating. The best pollinator for a hardy American variety called ('Ember'), developed at the University of Minnesota is the 'Toka,' a freestone with almost spicy flavor and brilliant red fruit. 'Toka' was developed in Canada from crosses of the American and apricot plum (*Prunus simoni*). In the prairie states and western Canada, the hybrids that carry strong resemblance to the native species include 'Bounty,' 'Manet,' and 'South Dakota.' In the Korean species *P. triflora*, cultivars such as 'Mandarin,' 'Ivanovka,' and others have been selec-

ted. Canadian and Japanese species produce the varieties 'Pembina,' 'Mina,' and 'Grenville.' The American and Japanese varieties, 'Radisson,' 'Underwood,' 'Red Wing,' and 'Superior' are notable.

The main commercial varieties (besides the native species and hybrids) are European (blue or common plums), Japanese or Oriental plums, and 'Damson.' Prunes are a type of European plum, with a high sugar content. 'Damson' plums come from England and are hardy in subzero temperatures. 'Green Gage' is of French origin, but its name is from an English family that imported and popularized the variety. Both varieties are self-pollinated.

'Stanley' is the best plum for the cold Midwest; 'Green Gage' is the second choice. 'Shiro' and 'Burbank' are the hardiest Japanese varieties, but they need 'Santa Rosa' or 'Methley' as pollinators.

The 'Methley and 'Mariposa' have a low chilling requirement and do best in the mild-winter areas.

European plums that are hardy to zone 3 and Japanese varieties that are less hardy (zone 5) are listed in Appendix tables 4 and 5.

Cherries

The hardiest cherries are selected varieties of the sand cherry (also called cherry-plum), such as 'Brooks,' 'Mando,' and 'Manmoor.' The Mongolian dwarf bush species known as *Prunus fruiticosa* produces 3-to-5-foot bushes with consistently heavy crops.

Of the sour and sweet cherries, the hardiest are the sour, or pie cherries. They grow from zone 4 to 9 and have the lowest chilling requirement. They are excellent garden trees, even smaller than sweet-cherry trees.

The sour cherry varieties, 'Meteor' and 'North Star,' developed at the University of Minnesota, are hardy semidwarfs, 8 to 10 feet tall. 'North Star' is used as a rootstock to dwarf varieties of sour and sweet cherries. 'Montmorency' is the favorite sour variety, followed by 'Early Richmond' and 'English Morello.' Duke cherries, a cross between sweet and sour cherries, are only as hardy as their sweet-cherry parent. They are self-fruitful, and they can pollinate some sweet cherries.

The best substitute for the sweet cherry in the north is the Nanking species. Two selected varieties with excellent fruits are 'Drilea' and 'Orient.' The hardiest true sweet cherries are 'Emperor,' 'Francis,' 'Hedelfingen,' and 'Napoleon,' but 'Emperor' and 'Napoleon' will not pollinate each other.

Apricots

Apricot trees are hardy, but they bloom so early that their flowers are almost always destroyed by frost. Nevertheless, considerable work has been done on the apricot by the experiment stations in the North, and the varieties 'Scout,' 'Sing,' 'Robust,' and 'Ninguta' are good for certain districts in the prairie states and Canada. 'Moongold' and 'Sungold,' developed at the University of Minnesota and relased in 1961, adapted to zone 3.

If you want a good shade tree and are willing to take a chance on never getting a crop of apricots, try the 'Large Early Montgamet.' It has sweet flesh and aroma, and it contains an edible seed, somewhat like an almond, inside its pit or stone.

In mild-winter areas of little winter chilling, 'Newcastle,' 'Nugget,' 'Perfection,' 'Redsweet,' and the 'Royal Blenheim' adapt. 'Royal Blenheim' is the most commonly sold apricot in the early market. 'Reeves' has the lowest chilling requirement.

Peaches

The hardiest peaches survive even if the ground freezes and snow stays on the ground all winter. Wherever late frost regularly occurs, early-blooming varieties must be avoided. Those varieties that have "haven" in their name derive from the South Haven Experiment Station in Michigan and are very cold-resistant; some endure -20°F, although this low temperature may cause some bud damage. 'South Haven,' 'Sunhaven,' and 'Redhaven' are examples of the cold-resistant types. 'Hale-haven,' 'Early Crawford,' 'Giant Elberta,' 'Halberta,' and 'Indian Cling' are the best kinds for the coldest areas of eastern Colorado, Nebraska, southern South Dakota, Iowa, and southern Wisconsin. According to the David Burgess Seed and Plant Company of Galesburg, Michigan, 'Marquette' "will grow and ripen fruits farther north than any other peach." 'Marquette' originated on the northern peninsula of Michigan.

The varieties with the lowest chilling requirement and the most dependability in the warm-winter areas include 'Babcock,' 'Bonita,' and 'Ventura.' The fruiting/flowering varieties 'Saturn' and 'Double Delight' were developed from the Chinese flat peach (Peen-to) and thrive in Southern California. The 'Southland' variety, developed by the U.S. Department of Agriculture, adapts to southern Florida.

Peaches that can be grown easily in the wide area between zones 9 and 4 are listed in Appendix table 6.

Nectarines

Nectarines are smooth-skinned peaches with smaller, sweeter fruits. The hardiest varieties are 'Boston,' 'Fuzzless,' 'Berta,' 'Garden State,' and 'Red Chief.' Two new varieties that thrive in southern California are 'Pioneer' and 'Silver Lode.' 'Silver Lode' ripens first in July; 'Pioneer' is ready the last week of July. The older varieties are white-fleshed and clingstone; the newer ones are yellow-fleshed and freestone.

The new natural dwarfs now available include 'Golden Prolific' (yellow-fleshed) and 'Silver Prolific' (white-fleshed). Both are freestones that ripen at midseason. Burgess lists a dwarf nectarine that is "hardy in the North." Armstrong Nurseries recently introduced a natural dwarf nectarine, cousin of the famous 'Bonanza' peach. It is called 'Nectarina,' and the shiny, large fruits are rich red overlaid with yellow.

Appendix

TABLE 1 APPLE SPUR VARIETIES

(as listed by Brooks and Olmo in the
Register of New Fruit and Nut Varieties.)

'Oregon Spur Delicious' — Bud sport of 'Red King Delicious.' Discovered 1966 in Oregon. Plant Patent 2816, assigned Van Well Nursery, Inc., Wenatchee, Washington. Fruit resembles parent, except colors earlier.

'Skyspur' — Bud sport of 'Skyline Supreme.' Discovered 1957 in Delaware. Introduced by Bountiful Ridge Nurseries, Princess Anne, Maryland. Fruit resembles parent.

'Atwood Spur Delicious' — Bud sport of 'Delicious.' Discovered 1956 in Washington. Introduced 1967, assigned to Yakima Valley Nursery, Wenatchee, Washington. Fruit resembles parent, except colors earlier with darker blush or solid red.

'Elliot Spur Golden' — Bud sport of 'Golden Delicious.' Discovered in 1962 in Washington. Introduced in 1964 by M. W. Elliot, Wapato, Washington. Fruit resembles parent.

'Empress Spur Golden' — Bud sport of 'Golden Delicious.' Discovered in 1962 in Washington. Introduced 1965, assigned to Columbia Basin Nursery, Quincy, Washington. Fruit resembles parent.

'Starkspur Lodi' — Bud sport of 'Lodi.' Discovered 1960 in Washington. Introduced 1964, assigned Stark Brothers Nurseries and Orchard Company, Louisiana, Missouri. Patent Pending. Fruit resembles parent.

'Stark Krimson Delicious' — Bud sport 'of Delicious.' Discovered 1953 in Washington. Introduced 1962. Plant Patent 1930, assigned to Stark Brothers Nurseries and Orchard Company, Louisiana, Missouri. Fruit similar to parent, except colors earlier.

'Starkspur Winesap' — Bud sport of 'Winesap.' Discovered in Washington. Introduced 1963. Plant Patent 2313, assigned to Stark Brothers Nurseries and Orchard Company, Louisiana, Missouri. Fruit similar to parent.

'Miller Sturdy Spur Delicious' — ('Miller Spur,' 'Miller Spur Delicious'). Bud sport of 'Starking Delicious.' Discovered 1957 in West Virginia. Introduced 1963 by Hill Top Orchards and Nurseries, Hartford, Michigan. Plant Patent 2433. Fruit similar to parent, except color — dark, solid-red.

'Clawson Spur' — Bud sport of 'Starking Delicious.' Originated 1936 in Washington. Introduced 1958 by O. T. Clawson, Chelan, Washington. Fruit resembles parent.

'Frazier Goldenspur' — Bud sport of 'Golden Delicious.' Discovered 1961 in Washington. Introduced 1963 by Carlton Nursery Company, Forest Grove, Oregon. Fruit resembles parent.

TABLE 2   APPLE VARIETIES

NAME	SIZE	FLESH	SKIN COLOR	SEASON
'Anoka'	medium	tender	red	early
'Beverly Hills'	small	tender	striped red	early
'Cortland'	large	juicy	striped red	early
'Delicious'	large	juicy	striped red	late
'Duchess'	medium	tender	striped red	early
'Golden Delicious'	medium large	juicy	clear yellow	mid
'Greening'	large	tender	green	late
'Grimes' Golden'	medium	firm	clear yellow	late
'Haralson'	large	juicy	red	late
'Jonathan'	medium large	juicy	red	mid
'Lodi'	large	crisp	bright yellow	early
'McIntosh'	medium large	tender	bright red	mid
'Northern Spy'	large	juicy	striped red	very late
'Rome Beauty'	large	crisp	red	late
'Starking'	large	juicy	red	late
'Stayman Winesap'	large	tender	red	late
'Tropical Beauty'	large	tender	red	late
'Wealthy'		juicy		early
'White Pearmain'	medium large	tender	pale green	mid
'Yellow Newtown'	medium	firm	greenish yellow	late
'Winter Banana'	large	tender	pink	mid
'Yellow Transparent'	large	tender	yellow	early

TABLE 3   PEAR VARIETIES

NAME	SIZE	FLESH	SKIN COLOR	SEASON	SUSCEPTIBILITY TO FIRE BLIGHT
'Anjou'	large	melting	green	late	susceptible
'Bartlett'	large	buttery	yellow	mid	very susceptible
'Bosc'	large	buttery	dark yellow	late	susceptible
'Clapp Favorite'	large	melting	pale yellow	early	susceptible
'Comice'	very large	melting	greenish yellow	late	susceptible
'Duchess'	very large	buttery	greenish yellow	late	moderately resistant
'Gorham'	large	buttery	yellow	late	susceptible
'Hovey'	small	melting	pale yellow	late	susceptible
'Kieffer'	small	gritty	greenish yellow	late	very resistant
'Magness'	medium	buttery	yellow	mid	resistant
'Moonglow'	large	buttery	yellow	early	resistant
'Seckel'	small	buttery	brown	mid	resistant
'Starking Delicious'	large	buttery	yellow	mid	very resistant
'Starkrimson'	medium	buttery	yellow	early	susceptible
'Tyson'	medium	melting	yellow	early	resistant
'Winter Helis'	medium	buttery	yellow green	very late	susceptible

TABLE 4   EUROPEAN PLUM VARIETIES

NAME	SIZE	SKIN COLOR	FLESH COLOR	SEASON	POLLINATION
'Damson'	small	blue	amber	mid	self
'Green Gage'	medium	yellow-green	pale yellow	mid	self
'Italian'	medium	dark blue	yellow	mid	self
'President'	large	dark purple	yellow	late	needs
'Stanley'	large	bluish purple	greenish yellow	late	self
'Tragedy'	medium	dark purple	yellow green	early	needs

TABLE 5   JAPANESE PLUMS

NAME	SIZE	SKIN COLOR	FLESH COLOR	SEASON	POLLINATION
'Apex'	medium	dark red	cream	early	needs
'Beauty'	medium	crimson	amber	early	self
'Burbank'	large	red	yellow	mid	needs
'Burmosa'	large	yellow	amber	early	needs
'Duarte'	large	red	red	late	needs
'Elephant Heart'	large	red	ruby	late	needs
'Formosa'	large	yellow	yellow	early	needs
'Kelsey'	large	yellow	yellow	late	needs
'Mariposa'	large	reddish purple	dark red	mid	needs
'Redheart'	medium	red	red	mid	needs
'Santa Rosa'	large	crimson	yellow	early	self
'Satsuma'	medium	dark red	dark red	mid	needs
'Shiro'	small	yellow	yellow	mid	needs
'Sierra'	medium	red purple	amber	mid	self
'Wickson'	large	yellowish red	yellow	mid	needs

TABLE 6 PEACH VARIETIES

NAME	FLESH COLOR	CLING OR FREESTONE	SEASON
'Babcock'	white	free	early
'Bonita'	yellow	free	mid
'Double Delight'	yellow	free	early
'Early Crawford'	yellow	free	mid
'Elberta'	yellow	free	mid
'Fay Elberta'	yellow	free	mid
'Giant Elberta'	yellow	free	early
'Halberta'	yellow	free	mid
'Hale'	yellow	free	mid
'Halehaven'	yellow	free	mid
'Indian Cling'	yellow streaked with red	cling	late
'Marquette'	white	free	mid
'Rio Oso Gem'	yellow	free	late
'Saturn'	yellow	free	mid
'Sims'	yellow	cling	late
'Southland'	yellow	free	mid
'Ventura'	yellow	free	early

TABLE 7   CITRUS BLOOMING AND FRUITING BY MONTH

	JAN.	FEB.	MAR.	APR.	MAY	JUNE	JULY	AUG.	SEP.	OCT.	NOV.	DEC.
ORANGES												
'Washington Navel' ⎫	⊕	⊕	⊕	○	○							⊕
'Robertson Navel' ⎭												
'Summer Navel'			□	□	⊕	○	○	○	○			
'Valencia'	○	⊕	⊕	⊕	○	○	○	○	○	○	○	○
'Blood' ('Tarocco')			□	⊕	⊕	○	○	○	○	○		
TANGOR												
'Temple'		□	⊕	⊕	⊕	○						
'Dweet'			□	□	⊕	○	○	○				
MANDARIN												
(Tangerines)												
'Owari Satsuma'	○	○	○	□	□	□						○
'Dancy'		○	⊕	⊕	⊕	○	○					
'Clementine'	○	○	⊕	⊕	⊕	○	○					
'Kara'			□	⊕	⊕	○						
'Kinnow'	○	○	⊕	⊕	⊕	○	○	○	○	○	○	○
SOUR MANDARIN												
'Calamondin'	○	○	⊕	⊕	⊕	○	○	⊕	⊕	⊕	○	○
'Rangpur'	⊕	○	○	○	⊕	⊕	⊕	○	○	○	⊕	⊕
TANGELO												
'Minneola'	○	○	○	⊕	⊕	⊕	○	○				
'Sampson'			□	□	⊕	○	○	○	○			
LEMONS												
All	⊕	⊕	⊕	⊕	⊕	⊕	⊕	⊕	⊕	⊕	⊕	⊕
LIMES												
'Bearss'	○	○	○	⊕	⊕	○	○	⊕	⊕	⊕	⊕	⊕
'Mexican'	⊕	⊕	○	○	○	○	○	⊕	⊕	⊕	⊕	⊕
GRAPEFRUIT												
All	○	○	⊕	□	□					○	○	○
KUMQUAT												
'Nagami'	○	○	○	○	○	⊕	□	□	□	○	○	○

□ = flower
○ = fruit
⊕ = flower and fruit

TABLE 8 SPACING OF ESPALIERS		
Single Cordons	**Distance Apart (Feet)**	**Rows (Feet)**
APPLES		
'EM IX'	2	6–10
'EM I, II, VII'	2½	8–10
PEARS		
'Anger C'	2	6–10
'Anger A'	2½	8–10
Palmette		
APPLES		
'EM IX'	4	10
'EM IV, VII	12	8
'EM II'	15	8
PEARS		
'Anger C'	3	10
'Anger A'	4	10
Informal		
APRICOTS, PEACHES, PLUMS	14	10

TABLE 9   NUMBER OF PLANTS POSSIBLE PER ACRE

Space Required (Feet)	
2 X 5	4,356
2 X 10	2,178
4 X 5	2,178
4 X 10	1,089
5 X 5	1,742
5 X 10	871
10 X 10	435
10 X 12	363
10 X 15	290
10 X 20	217
20 X 20	108
40 X 40	27

TABLE 10 SPRAY AND DUST SCHEDULE

APPLE

Time of Application	Insect or Disease	Treatment	Amount/2 Gals. Water	Remarks
When tree is dormant	Scale insects Mite eggs Aphid eggs	Winter oil emulsion plus Diazinon 50% wettable powder	5-1/4 fl. oz. 1/3 oz.	Thorough application to trunks and limbs is necessary to obtain control.
Green-tip stage	Scab	Captan 50% wettable powder or Dodine 65% wettable powder	3 tbsp. 1 tbsp.	Repeat at pink-bud stage if weather is wet.
Pink-bud stage	Powdery mildew	Dinocap 48% liquid Karathane	1/2 tsp.	Add wetting agent to ensure penetration of spray. Two additional applications (applied with codling-moth sprays) may be necessary.
Full bloom	Fire blight	Streptomycin 17% wettable powder	As manufacturer directs	Three applications (full bloom, petal fall and late secondary bloom) are usually needed.
When all flower petals have fallen	Codling moth Aphid	Sevin 50% wettable powder plus Diazinon 50% wettable powder	2/3 oz. 1/6 oz.	Make a second treatment twenty-five days after the first treatment. A third treatment may be necessary in late June and a fourth during the second week of August.
June, or on appearance	Woolly apple Aphid	Diazinon 50% wettable powder	1/6 oz.	Repeat applications as aphids appear. If the combination treatments are applied for codling moths and aphids in June, treatment may not be necessary. Do not apply malathion within three days of harvest or diazinon within fourteen days of harvest.
When mites appear on leaves	Red spider mites	Kelthane 18-1/2% emulsive	2 tsp.	Do not apply Kelthane within seven days of harvest.

PEAR

Time of Application	Insect or Disease	Treatment	Amount/2 Gals. Water	Remarks
When tree is dormant	Scale insects, mite eggs	Use same treatment as for apples		Thorough application to trunks and limbs is necessary to obtain control. If the winter oil emulsion plus diazinon or malathion treatment is delayed until bud swell, it will also control pear psylla.
Start at 10% bloom. Repeat at five-day intervals until all bloom is over (especially during rainy weather)	Fire blight	Streptomycin 17% wettable powder	As manufacturer directs	Prune out blighted branches; cut back 15 inches into healthy wood. Sterilize all cuts and shears or saws each time with 1 part Lysol, 10 parts water.
When all flower petals have fallen	Codling moth Pear psylla	Sevin 50% wettable powder	2/3 oz.	Remarks under codling moth on apples apply to pears. Sevin will control immature forms of pear psylla and pear-leaf blister mite.
When mites appear on leaves	Red spider mites	Kelthane 18-1/2% emulsive	2 tsp.	Do not apply Kelthane within fourteen days of harvest.

APRICOT

Time of Application	Insect or Disease	Treatment	Amount/2 Gals. Water	Remarks
When tree is dormant (January or February)	Scale insects	Use same treatment as for apples		Thorough application to trunks and limbs is necessary to obtain control. Applications of winter oil emulsion plus diazinon at this time will also control twig borer.
When flower buds show red	Brown rot	Captan 50% wettable powder	3 tbsp.	

CHERRY

Time of Application	Insect or Disease	Treatment	Amount/2 Gals. Water	Remarks
When tree is dormant	Scale insects, mite eggs, aphid eggs	Use same treatment as for apples		Thorough application to trunks and limbs is necessary to obtain control.
After petals fall	Black cherry, aphid	Diazinon 50% wettable powder	1/6 oz.	Apply spray when aphids first appear. If spray is delayed, aphids will be difficult to control. Do not apply malathion within three days or diazinon within ten days of harvest.
When slugs appear on leaves	Cherry slug		1/6 oz.	Cherry slug is readily killed by applications of any dust such as hydrated lime or sulfur. Do not apply malathion within three days of harvest.

PEACH, NECTARINE

Time of Application	Insect or Disease	Treatment	Amount/2 Gals. Water	Remarks
November 15 to December 15 (or as leaves are falling)	Peach blight (coryneum and leaf curl)	Captan 50% wettable powder	As manufac- turer directs	Cover each bud with spray.
When tree is dormant (January or February)	Scale insects, mite eggs	Use same treatment as for apples		Thorough application to trunks and limbs is necessary to obtain control. Applications of winter oil emulsion plus diazinon at this time will also control twig borer.
Before buds begin to swell	Leaf curl only	Captan 50% wettable powder Dodine (cyprex)	3 tbsp. As manufac- turer directs	Needed only when November 15 to December 15 peach-blight spray has been omitted.
Pink-bud stage	Brown rot	Captan 50% wettable powder	3 tbsp.	If weather is wet, repeat at full bloom.
When 90% of flower petals have fallen	Twig borer	Sevin 50% wettable powder or Diazinon 50% wettable powder	2/3 oz. 1/3 oz.	The larvae of this insect cause "wormy" fruit. More treatments may be necessary when the fruit begins to ripen. Do not apply Sevin within seven days, or diazinon within twenty days of harvest.
Mid-May to early June	Twig borer, oriental fruit moth	Use same treatment as for twig borer (above)		
When mites appear on leaves	Red spider mites	Kelthane 18-1/2% emulsive	2 tsp.	Do not apply Kelthane within four- teen days of harvest.

PRUNE, PLUM

Time of Application	Insect or Disease	Treatment	Amount/2 Gals. Water	Remarks
When tree is dormant	Scale insects mite eggs aphid eggs	Use same treatment as for apples		Thorough application to trunks and limbs is necessary to obtain control. Applications of winter oil emulsion plus diazinon at this time will also control twig borer.
Popcorn stage	Brown rot	Captan 50% wettable powder	3 tbsp.	If weather is wet, repeat at full bloom.
When 90% of flower petals have fallen	Twig borer	Use same treatment as for peaches		The larvae of this insect cause "wormy" fruit. More treatments may be necessary about May 20 and when fruit begins to ripen (observe waiting periods).
When aphids appear on leaves	Mealy plum Louse	Diazinon 50% wettable powder	1/6 oz.	Do not apply diazinon within ten days of harvest.
When mites appear on leaves	Red spider mites	Kelthane 18-1/2% emulsive	2 tsp.	Do not apply Kelthane within seven days of harvest. Do not repeat applications within thirty days.

NAVELS, VALENCIAS, GRAPEFRUITS, LEMONS

Time of Application	Insect or Disease	Treatment	Amount/2 Gals. Water	Remarks
All year except during bloom period	Scale insects	Diazinon 50% wettable powder	1/6 oz.	Thorough coverage is necessary for control. For red and yellow scale preferred timing is during immediate postbloom or before fruit is infested. Do not apply within ten days of picking.
When mites appear on leaves (use magnifying glass)	Citrus red mite	Kelthane 18-1/2% emulsive	2 tsp.	Do not apply Kelthane within seven days of picking.
When aphids appear on leaves	Aphid	Diazinon 50% wettable powder	1/6 oz.	Do not apply during bloom period or within ten days of picking.
When mealy bugs appear on leaves and twigs	Mealybugs	Diazinon 50% wettable powder	1/6 oz.	Do not apply during bloom period or within ten days of picking.
At end of petal fall	Thrips	Diazinon 50% wettable powder	1/6 oz.	Do not apply during bloom period or within ten days of picking.
As required except during bloom	Orangeworms	Sevin 5% dust		Apply uniformly but lightly. Do not apply within five days of picking.

Index

Note: Italicized page references indicate illustrations.